Dog Bre

C000088453

By
"Wildfowler"

Vintage Dog Books
Home Farm
44 Evesham Road
Cookhill, Alcester
Warwickshire
B49 5LJ

www.vintagedogbooks.com

© Read Books 2005
This book is copyright and may not be
reproduced or copied in any way without
the express permission of the publisher in writing.

ISBN No. 978-1-84664-997-4

Published by Vintage Dog Books 2005
Vintage Dog books is an imprint of Read Books

British Library Cataloguing-in-Publication Data
A catalogue record for this book is available
from the British Library.

Vintage Dog Books
Home Farm
44 Evesham Road
Cookhill, Alcester
Warwickshire
B49 5LJ

By " WILDFOWLER."

DOG BREAKING.

A Practical Treatise on the Training and Management
of Shooting Dogs.

(ILLUSTRATED.)

With a Chapter on

POINTS OF SPORTING DOGS.

By Fred Gresham.

———

LONDON
PUBLISHED BY THE BURLINGTON PUBLISHING COMPANY, LIMITED,
74 77 TEMPLE CHAMBERS, BOUVERIE STREET, E.C.

1915.

RETRIEVED NEARLY A MILE AWAY.

DOG BREAKING.

By "WILDFOWLER."

In accordance with the wishes of very many of my readers, I produce my "Dog Breaking" in book form. I will try to be as brief as possible, so as to bring my information before public in as concise a form as convenient, but the matter requires now and then a good deal of explanation, and I crave my readers' forgiveness if sometimes, in the heat of my narrative, I happen to launch forth into some anecdote in connection with my subject. Such things are unavoidable, presumably, when a fit of the "cacoethes scribendi" comes upon a fellow.

Now to business.

The first portion of my subject will be what I should call—

PUPPYHOOD EDUCATION.

Mrs. Glass—the inimitable Mrs. Glass—in her never-to-be-forgotten advice with regard to cooking hares, says: "First catch your hare." I say, with equally striking truth, "If you want to break a puppy, first get one," and I add to it, "And, above all, take care that it be a good one."

And this, I must explain, has no reference whatsoever to his personal appearance. Of course, if he is good looking, as well as promising for work, all the better, but above all things sporting qualities are a sine qua non, or you will waste your time over a most unlikely pupil. The young dog should be well bred, i.e., from sporting stock, well made, intelligent, good-tempered,

healthy, and good-nosed. The latter you can always
find out in the most summary manner by taking your
dog into a field under wind, some considerable distance
from a lump of horseflesh, for instance, which you have
got placed there on purpose, but completely hidden. The
puppy who first acknowledges the "scent" and goes up
towards the spot will be the keenest-nosed performer of
the lot.

That being settled, and everything else satisfactory
as regards the make and general health and intelligence
of the puppy, the sooner you take him in hand the better; but he must, of course, be sufficiently developed to
stand the fatigue and worry, and he must have done with
the preliminary foolishness of puppyhood. If not, he
will not understand you, but will, as likely as not, roll
on his back and playfully bark at you, or attempt to
seize your hand in fun when you want to "drop" him.
Therefore, you should take him in hand only when he
begins to be sober-minded. Take him out with you,
then, on the roads, on a leash at first, and make him
follow you; if he objects, do not drag him along, but try
if a piece of biscuit will make him do so. If he is still
too shy, you must couple him to a steady old dog, and
walk with them about the yard, until the puppy sees
that you mean no harm. Then take him out, and as
soon as he follows well teach him to drop, at first by
gently forcing him down and keeping him there. When
he has done so and remained steady several times, teach
him to do so upon your lifting your hand from the distance of a few yards. To effect this, peg him down,
then raise your hand and call out "Drop," then walk
away from him backwards, going to him and forcing
him down every time he gets up, and keep your hand up
until he remains down well, without attempting to follow you.

After a few lessons of that sort, the slip should be
removed, and the dog should be repeatedly "dropped"
by voice and hand when running about, say, in a dry
meadow. The moment a puppy drops readily, half the
trouble of breaking him is over. I have known dogs
take to it very kindly, others gave a deal of trouble; but
as a rule, two or three days' constant work will effect the
object with the most obstinate puppy. The whip should
be resorted to only if the dog is very wilful and obsti-

STEADY UNDER TEMPTATION.

nate, and then it should be used gently. Any breaker can teach a dog to drop in two hours by simply "flogging it" into him, but I don't call that training a dog, I call it breaking his spirit, amd he will not retain what he has been taught in such a short time, simply because it is not impressed upon his mind by habit, but he was simply compelled to obey by sheer cruelty and dread of punishment. A dog of that sort will break out again the next day, and require harder punishment, perhaps, or he will be so cowed by that one man that he will sulkily drop to him and no one else. I repeat it, this is not breaking. A well-broken dog should act for his new master—when the latter has put him through the usual drill—as readily as he used to act for his trainer. But I will harp on that string again by-and-by.

The puppy, then, having been taught to downcharge to hand and to voice, is on a fair way to absolute control. He should then be introduced to horses, cattle, sheep, pigs, fowls, ducks, pigeons, etc., and all attempts to chase should be repressed, and, if persisted in wilfully, should be checked with some severity, until the puppy can be trusted not to notice anything out of the common, and not to chase cats or other domestic animals.

Some dogs readily enter into all that sort of thing; others delight in mischief, and these latter are not always the worst by any means in the long run; therefore great patience should be exercised. Indeed, a man who is not endowed with that virtue should certainly not attempt dog breaking in any form or shape.

"Stonehenge"—the infallible "Stonehenge" himself—advises, mirabile dictu, "pulling a dog by the ears if not complying with your orders." A more mischievous direction could not have been given by the veriest tyro. A dog should never be pulled by the ear, and I can only wonder at such an edict issuing from the pen of the Editor of "The Field." I say emphatically, no dog of any breed should ever have his ears pulled, on any pretence whatsoever, and if a keeper or breaker of mine were to be caught by me in the act, I should discharge him on the spot without the slightest hesitation. Moreover, no dog should be struck with a whip or stick across the face. Its eyes might be hurt permanently, and precious little practical training that would be. To correct a dog, the trainer should hold it tight by its col-

lar, and punish it with a whip over the body, and he
should never strike in anger. If a man cannot control
his own temper, he is not fit to be a breaker. I have
seen a man seize a dog by the nape of the neck, fling it
about, and dash it to the ground, and then, whilst holding him there, kick him with all his might. That is
neither humane nor sensible, and certainly not training.
Above all things, a dog inclined to be nervous should
never be struck when trained to the report of a gun. A
dog who is slightly afraid at first of the report will be
made a confirmed gun-shy beast if he is struck when
starting at the noise. Yet some men get hold of a
frightened puppy, lather him, and shout: "What are
you afraid of, you fool?"

The greater fool of the two is, in that case, the man,
I trow.

The best plan to prevent gun-shyness in puppies is to
crack a pistol as a signal for meal-times, until they
come to look upon the report as a most welcome incident.
A few shots during their meals will also accustom them
thoroughly not to mind the noise. Older puppies, who
have been neglected in that respect, should be taken in
hand carefully, if they are worth the trouble, and I have
found that killing a bird to such a dog will bring him
round quicker than any other method, provided he be
allowed to mouth the bird. As a rule, however, I dis-
card gun-shy dogs at once, as I take it that the first
condition of success with a puppy is that he should be
bold. I should never care to undertake myself curing
a gun-shy dog—my contempt for such a beast would not
allow me to do it justice—and I think in many cases
that it is a mere waste of time to take in hand such an
enterprise; in this way, that granted you cure the dog
for a while, he is always an uncertain dog to rely upon,
and may break out again at the slightest chance.
"Show" puppies (i.e., of show stock for generations) are
very apt to be gun-shy. Indeed, many sporting (heaven
save the mark!) dogs are now exhibited—and, indeed,
some well-known winners—are gun-shy, and I venture
to say that there is something deplorable in that fact.

Howbeit, we cannot alter such facts. If a man finds
that a perfectly worthless brute—for sport—will bring
him in money on the show-bench, he will show him, win
prizes with him, put him at stud, and perpetuate his

gun-shyness; but what does that matter to him? That is the way things are looked at by several persons whom I could name if I chose.

But let us return to our not-gun-shy puppy. It is a very good plan to encourage puppies from an early age to look upon hares and rabbits with indifference. For this reason, a fenced-in and wired enclosure where rabbits are allowed to breed ad libitum is a very good adjunct to a large kennel. Failing which, a wood swarming with rabbits which the puppy may be shown in numbers, morning and evening, at their feeding time, when they are out on the stubbles—is an excellent thing. A puppy who gets the chance of seeing twenty rabbits twice a day, and is chided if he notices them, soon comes to walk amongst them with indifference. In America, rabbits are kept in wired-in enclosures in front of the dog kennels, so that the puppies may get used to them—a very excellent plan, which might be here copied with advantage.

Once a puppy can be dropped readily, at any distance, and he is well in hand for fur, he will do, as far as his preliminary education goes, and, therefore, we may now take him in hand for —

POINTER AND SETTER FIELD BREAKING.

To begin with, though my opinion runs contrary to that of several authorities, I beg to say that, most decidedly, springtime is the season par excellence for entering pointers and setters to game, and I will, by-and-by, give my reasons therefor.

In some books the intending breaker is advised to teach quartering to his young dog where there is no game. How a dog can learn to quarter without knowing what he is to look for is one of those mysteries which "no fellah can understand." My plan is different to that, and is very simple withal.

First, if you have a broken dog, run your puppy with him. The broken dog will begin quartering at once, and the puppy will readily enough, in nine cases out of ten, in fact, take the hint. Animals cannot converse, but they understand each other all the same, and the young dog will soon know that there is something in the

wind. At first, he will follow the old one aimlessly,
more for the fun of running after him than for any other
motive, not knowing what is up. But let the old dog
get a point, and the young one will soon have all his
sporting instinct to the fore. He will possibly, at first,
take the point, run in, and " knock 'em up "; indeed, if
he is a high-couraged youngster, it is very probable that
he will do so, but he will be none the worse for it. Anyhow, whether he stood well or ran in, it does not matter,
so far, but he certainly will look for more birds afterwards, and, if properly handled, will get on all right in
his quartering, but great care should be exercised. Thus,
always be careful to give him the wind. Nothing so
demoralises a young dog—or an old dog, for the matter
of that—as flushing by no fault of his. But, being
given the wind, the young dog should be slipped quietly,
so as to give him a chance. Eventually he may get too
bold and "get away." but, if he is well under control,
he will keep his eye on you and bear off at a tangent if
he sees you going off too at a tangent. If he does not do
so according to your own motions, drop him, then call
him to you, drop him again when he is thirty yards off,
and wave him off in another direction, and repeat this
until he follows your every motion, and whichever side
towards which you walk he must at once turn that way
also. "Breaking fence " is likely to be the next trouble
if the puppy is very bold ; but if you keep your eye on
him, and the moment he nears the fence you wave him
off in the opposite direction, walking that way yourself
and even turning your back to him, he will be likely to
take the hint, and not offend much in that respect ; but
should he wilfully break fence you should get up to it as
quickly as possible, drop him, and drag him back to the
field where he should have remained, and punish him if
he repeats the offence.

Some puppies with a dash of hound in their blood
dearly love pottering about fences. This is a great
fault, and it requires very patient breaking. But
walking the puppy along fences on a leash, and giving
him a cut of the whip every time he offers to poke his
nose in the fence will work wonders. At the same time,
" Rome was not built in a day," and patience should be
exercised in this matter. Above all things, do not run
your puppy with another dog unless the latter is perfect.

A LAVERACK SETTER STANCH ON FUR.

for if by a fluke the old one commits himself, the young one will join in, and it will take a great deal of work and trouble to make him understand that it was wrong.

If you have no perfect old dog to rely upon, it is vastly preferable to train the youngster by himself, and I do not mind saying that my plan to induce a puppy to quarter readily is simplicity itself, though possibly not my own invention. I simply take the young dog out where I know I can get a shot—if in the spring, when shooting is over, I can always find some well-known barren pair, or an old cock—and as soon as we walk up to the birds I kill one. The puppy is then allowed to have a good smell at the spot the bird rose from, and then, as we walk up towards the dead bird, he is waved on, and the scent coming hot to him, nine times out of ten he will "point dead" on the spot. I then pick up the bird, bring it to him, and let him bury his nose in its warm feathers. Sometimes one such lesson is sufficient, the puppy afterwards needing but little encouragement and looking for game readily.

With regard to pointing, I have bred setters and pointers which pointed when less than four months old. Pointing can be taught to any dog, but cataleptic pointing is not taught, and cannot be taught. It is a natural propensity, and is bred into the dog. The difference between trained pointing and cataleptic pointing is plain. The trained pointing of a Clumber, or of a Sussex (some are broken to do that), is vastly different from the cataleptic pointing of the setter or pointer who is knocked "all of a heap" by the scent, and is there heaving his chest and nearly dropping his eyes out with his "fit." I take it that a well-bred pointer or setter puppy should show that quality more or less early in his career, but that to have any great success with him he should early show it when brought on game. On the other hand, it should not be so strongly cultivated as to make the dog a false pointer. Some men drop their puppies whenever they come to a point, as soon as they take it. If it turns out that there is game, well and good, but if every time a puppy draws himself up he has not a second or two given him to find out whether he is "all right" or not, but is dropped at once by his breaker, "for fear he should make a mistake" (the usual excuse), then, possibly, the dog will grow into the habit of dropping to every scent, false or true, strong or stale, and he will give no end of bother with his false pointing.

Now, false pointing in a partridge country, although a nuisance, is not nearly so troublesome a bad habit as on the moors. Imagine, on a hot day in August, having to tramp half a mile or so a score of times to a dog who is, after all, only false pointing. The treat must be fully undergone to be fairly appreciated. No! I contend that when training a puppy on his points, he should within reasonable measure, be allowed to use his nose, and his brains. When he pulls up, give him time, and if he gradually stiffens and stands well, then go up to him gently, stand by him, and the moment the bird rises, drop him, and keep him down to wing (or even to gun, if you have fired a blank shot) tor two or three minutes at least. Never be in a hurry, and your dog won't get flurried. More dogs are spoilt by fussy men than through any other cause, and it is for that reason partly that I do not advocate breaking dogs during the shooting season. Imagine having a promising young setter flurried out of his "drop" by a greedy shot racing after a winged bird, and chasing it, with loud execrations, all round the unlucky puppy. I have seen such things times out of number, and for that reason I say emphatically, never undertake to break a dog unless you alone have control over him, and you are alone, in fact, with him. Solitude a deux is, then, a sine qua non, and, as you must not be tempted to make a "bag" when you are breaking a puppy, I say that spring time is the season wherein your operations should be conducted; and I trust my views and reasons will be endorsed by those of my readers who have practically undertaken breaking dogs.

The chief agent in breaking a pointer or setter puppy to game should not be the whip, as many men seem to think, but, on the other hand, the whip should not be done entirely without, as some other men seem to imagine. Broadly speaking, if a dog is at all inclined to be nervous, the whip will spoil him, and therefore it should not be used at all, but for very bold dogs it is an absolute necessity, not so much perhaps as an active means of punishment as a deterrent. At any rate, I would depreciate most earnestly any violent use of the whip. Thrashing a dog, as many men express it, is wrong. Two or three mild cuts whilst downcharging the dog will do him good, whereas a good licking, wildly administered, puzzles the dog, who is driven crazy with the pain, and henceforth will sneak away when punishment is likely to be administered to him, thus preventing his teaching from being successfully carried out. The check-rope is best thing in the world for training a dog, but it should be used systematically, patiently, and thoroughly. Now, why nine out of ten so-called dogs in the market are only half-broken lies simply in the fact that nine out of ten breakers do not know their work, or else, knowing it, shirk it, either through idleness or from some physical infirmity. I will explain my meaning.

Let us suppose a dashing young setter is in the hands of a middle-aged keeper to break. The dog getting away, say, repeatedly, riles the man, who, instead of carrying on the training programme to the letter—i.e., dragging the puppy back to the place he should have dropped it—every time he does wrong, loses his temper, swears at the dog, goes after him, gets hold of him, and gives him there and then a tremendous thrashing. This simply happens through the man losing his temper. Possibly, a dozen times already he had patiently checked the dog under various circumstances, and dragged him back to drop him, enforcing his orders mildly, but firmly. Now he has got exasperated, forgets himself, and by that unlucky thrashing may have made, henceforth, a perfect brute of your dog. The chief incentive to such conduct, however, lies in the fact that the breaker may labour under some physical infirmity, which prevents him from stooping readily enough to carry on his duties. It stands to reason that a man whose "knees are gone," as the saying goes, or who suffers from lumbago, rheumatism, et hoc genus omne, may be willing, but unable, to do justice to the breaking he has undertaken to carry out. Now, I make bold to say that in many cases, such is the reason why dogs are badly broken, and the other cases of non-success can be traced to sheer idleness. There are some men who will not "run after a dog," as they put it: but this attendance upon a dog in all his motions is absolutely necessary. Every time the dog does wrong he should be dropped as soon as possible, dragged back, and dropped again at the spot where he was when he was first ordered down and disobeyed the order, or disregarded his previous lessons. Thus, the puppy, let us say, for instance, after winding his birds and standing them for a second, has run in and put them up; he should be dragged back forcibly to the spot where he first pointed, and with the word "Drop" he should be dropped there and kept there for three or four minutes without moving. If he has chased the birds a cut or two of the whip and calling out "'Ware chase" whilst he is dropped, will do him good, if he stands punishment well; if not, the check-rope should be shaken, more or less violently, whilst the words are spoken to impress upon him what is required of him.

The great secret in all this is to repeat these lessons frequently. No dog can be broken quickly. Some dogs, of course, take to their work sooner than others, but all require practice, and this demands time and plenty of work on game.

When a puppy coming on birds attempts to run in, care should be taken not to jerk him violently down with the rope, with a view to steadying him and making him point them, for by so doing he may connect birds with punishment, and afterwards take to blinking. There is no doubt that blinking is a vice acquired through the cruel or injudicious treatment of the dog when he was first entered to game. It is one of the worst defects—if not the very worst—which a dog may have, and its cure, in many cases, is very doubtful, some dogs temporarily rid of this bad habit falling into it again in the most unaccountable manner at any time if disturbed by any loud noise, such as that made by a ploughman's whip, or a shot, when they are coming on point. In fact, evidently when the dog was first entered to birds he had been beaten or jerked about, head over heels, when he had attempted putting up his birds, and ever since he has come to dread a similar treatment whenever he gets on scent. Hence lies confirmed blinking. It can be cured in some instances, but, as a rule, a blinker is very unreliable. I know a good finder of game who has figured in a field trial prize list, but who could not stand being shot over, not from gun-shyness, as he was not afraid of the gun when not near birds, but of the whip when he got on his points, and that is one of the reasons why I have always insisted in many of my articles upon field trials being carried out as though one

AN OLD-FASHIONED SETTER.

was actually shooting over dogs. It may surprise some outsiders to hear—but it is, nevertheless, a fact—that some winners at field trials were gun-shy brutes totally unfit for real sport, and I contend that such a state of things is, to put it mildly, very disingenuous on these dogs' owners' part. But then the rules of the running are to blame. They should be framed so as to insure two shots being fired for every point taken by either of the dogs. Had this been done at every field trial I have attended, some dogs that I wot of who have taken honours there would have been put to most ignominious flight sooner or later.

It cannot be too strongly impressed upon the beginner that the temper of each dog must be studied if any good results are to be attained. No two dogs behave exactly alike under the very same circumstances. A bold dog requires a lot of talking (i.e., shouting) to, and some whip; a timid one should not be bullied or struck; and there are various grades intervening which call for no inconsiderable display of suavitor in modo, tempered with fortiter in re. Now, in the matter of teaching to point, let us imagine two puppies, possibly from the same litter, but one bold and the other timid. Of course, they are taken in hand separately, for certainly no good could come of working two such incongruous units together. Well, then, the bold one points; put your foot on his check-rope, so as to be ready to check him if he attempts to run in, and call out "Drop!" as loud as you can. Your voice will flush the birds, and if the dog drops to wing there and then, well and good; if not, you have him at your mercy, and can stop him and drag him back to drop him where he ought originally to have dropped.

So far, so good. But if the timid dog had been in hand, the same style of doing things would not have answered at all. For, when he first scented the birds, if you had called out "Drop!" in a stentorian tone of voice from behind him, it is ten to one that, frightened at your shout, and also bewildered by the rising of the birds, the dog would not have dropped at all, but would have slunk back to your heels, fearing he had done wrong. Therefore, for such a dog, even the check-rope should be used with care, and what I advise doing is: Have an iron ring tied to the end of his rope (which,

by the way, need not be longer than twenty yards), and
provide yourself with a sharp iron spike. As soon as the
timid dog winds his birds and steadies himself for his
point, thrust your spike through the check-rope ring
and drive it firmly with your foot into the ground, all
the while speaking gently to the dog, "To ho! Good
dog!" in a low, caressing tone of voice, then advance to
him, drop him, and go up towards the birds backwards,
keeping your hand up, and speaking to your dog all the
while. You can thereby control his every action, and
he will not be upset either by voice or by the whirr of
the wings. If he attempts to follow you, the rope will
check him, so altogether he is entirely controlled and in
a manner totally devoid of violence—a great point this
with a nervous puppy. The point over, the nervous
puppy should be made much of, and if a bird has been
shot he should be allowed a good sniff at it whilst it is
warm; but a bold puppy does not require too much of
that sort of thing, otherwise, should he see a bird fall, he
will want to run in and pick it up—a fault to be avoided
here, but which is looked upon as a great accomplishment by some "pot-hunters" on the Continent and in
America, where the loss of a winged bird is looked upon
as but little short of a national calamity.

As a matter of fact, therefore, it will be seen that the
check-rope is the multum-in-parvo of dog breaking.
Once the dog is thoroughly impressed with the convic-
tion that he is at all times completely under your
control, his education is in a very fair way of being
accomplished. Some men are great adepts in the art,
and will do wonders with but little game on which to
break their dogs; others, with thousands of acres swarming with feather and fur, can hardly turn out a satisfactory dog in a whole season. I may here say that the
man who "drinks," is out of the running altogether, and
such a man is worse than rank poison amongst your
dogs. I have always made it a rule amongst my own
men that the first case of insobriety entails discharge on
the spot, and I found the strict carrying out of that rule
most beneficial. A drunken man is simply a man mad
for the time being, and an owner must be very simple
indeed who allows a madman at any time to play his
pranks amongst his dogs.

A breaker who knows his work and who is a total ab-

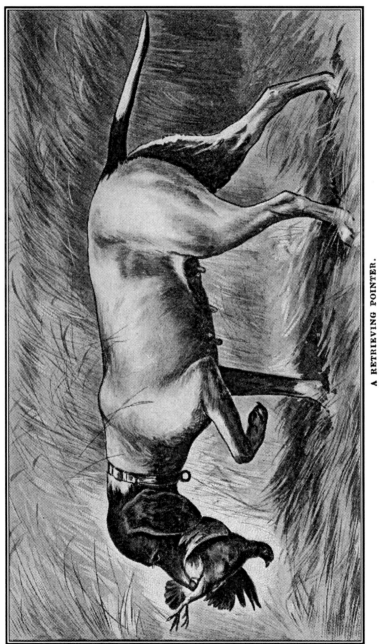

A RETRIEVING POINTER.

stainer is invaluable in a kennel, but there are very few men who join the two requisites. Now, a good breaker, even where there is but little game, if he is willing and industrious, will turn out first-rate working dogs. It is a mistake to suppose that a lot of game is wanted to break a puppy. It is quite wrong, because the puppy gets bewildered by too much feather or fur. If a man can get a puppy on four or five brace of birds in one morning's work, he ought to be well satisfied, because every time he gets him on a point he can make the most of it, and duly impress upon the youngster what he ought to do and ought not to do under the circumstances, whereas if the training takes place in a spot swarming with game untoward and puzzling events may happen which will interfere with the tuition. Thus, if birds rise all round the puppy, he will be bothered, and the same thing will occur if a lot of hares jump out of their forms and scamper all over a bare field, almost inviting him to a run. On the other hand, when the dog is well-nigh broken, he cannot see too much of that sort of thing—but at the beginning things should be taken rather coolly, and I say that four or five points every morning will do wonders with a promising pupil. Frequently it will occur that, possibly for sheer love of mischief, a puppy who has hitherto behaved well to fur takes it into his head to chase. This should be checked at once, and means taken to repress the tendency without delay. If the land is open and without fences, the best plan is to look out for a hare in her form, and then fetch the dog for her, rigging him up with his collar and check-rope, so as to stop the chasing from the beginning. Some men are content with driving the iron rod through the ring at the end of the check-rope into the ground and let the dog do his worst—which inevitably ends in his turning a somersault when he reaches the end of his tether—but, as he may break his neck, or otherwise hurt himself, I fail to see the beauty of the arrangement, and I think that holding the rope himself is far more satisfactory on the breaker's part, because the dog feels at once the all-masterful power of the man over him, and is more inclined to give in than merely to mechanical resistance. Many lessons of the sort are required for a confirmed chaser, and he should also have the whip if he is very obstinate. In a district much intersected with

fences it is well to hunt a dog who is inclined to chase
with a check-rope and a stout oaken stick tied by its
middle at the end of the rope. If the dog behaves himself he won't feel much inconvenience from dragging
rope and stick, but should he bolt after fur through a
fence he will be sure to be brought to, more or less suddenly, by the stick catching sideways among the roots.
But, after all, early training in that matter is the thing.
If a puppy when very young is taken amongst a lot of
fur and well broken of them, he will never notice them
in after life, except he has a dash of hound in his blood,
in which case the thing looks bad.   I have known dogs
which could never be broken of fur.   Anyhow,
they would make a start after it, in spite of all
correction.

Bad example also may go a long way in the matter of
chasing.   Let a puppy see another dog chasing—especially if the latter is giving tongue—and it will indeed
be surprising if the puppy does not join in.   In fact, I
may say I have never known a puppy under such circumstances which did not chase more or less keenly.

It is desirable at first to avoid running a young setter
or pointer on French birds, because, owing to these
birds' nasty habit of running, they are apt to puzzle
puppies exceedingly at first; but that it is perfectly
feasible to break them on "Frenchmen" has been
proved to demonstration, not only in my own kennels
in Essex, but in several others which I could name,
where the shooting lessee has almost as many French
as English birds on his ground.   But once broken on
them there is, in the long run, this advantage—that
the dog is equal to anything.   Should he subsequently
be used for all-round sport, a running cock pheasant will
not disturb his equanimity, as, from old experience, he
will be used to that sort of thing.   Moreover, I think a
dog used to French birds gets to be far more cunning
than one who is not, and he will pin these birds down
when one not used to them will fail most ignominiously.
But the dog must on no account be a potterer.   If he
puts his nose to the ground he will lose all style.   He
should go about head well up and come upon them sharp
and swift, otherwise they will sneak away.   Indeed,
they often do, in spite of all care and style, and this is
very trying to a puppy, particularly if any thick hedges

are about and the birds get through them. In pairing time, however, French birds are much quieter, and I have often come upon brace after brace of a morning at such time without the slightest attempt being made by them at evading the dogs. If a puppy will persist in running in to shot and wing, the best plan is to have a tame bird pegged down in some grassy plot, where all its motions can readily be seen by the puppy. To avoid chafing the bird's legs, a piece of leather should be sewn around each leg, and two strings, one long and one short, should be tied to the leather. Peg the bird down with the short string, stretch the other string at full length, and let the bird get settled in its spot for at least ten minutes if the weather is very dry and there is but little wind, so as to give time to its scent to get fully developed, for it is necessary—notwithstanding views to the contrary—that the dog should know by nose as well as by sight that he is on game. Were it otherwise, a common chicken might answer the purpose. But this would not be the case. I know a man who once used a tame pigeon for that purpose, and his dog dropped readily to the pigeon, but whenever he afterwards came upon game he was off after it. Therefore, let the scent of the partridge be fully developed, then rig up your puppy with his collar and check-rope, and bring him on to the bird gently, giving him the full benefit of the wind if there be any. Of course, he will point and stand his bird at a more or less great distance, according to the power of his olfactory nerves and the strength of the scent. When he has been perfectly steady on point for a little while, pick up the long string, jerk it gently, when the bird will jump up in sight of the dog. If the puppy wishes to go in, check him at once, gently if he be gentle, but somewhat roughly if he is violently inclined to rush up, and if he persists use the whip moderately. Anyway, on no consideration let him give you the slip. For greater safety he might be pegged down first of all if he is known to be a thoroughly rough and determined youngster. He is thus at your mercy. When you have steadied him, fire a shot. The noise will startle both dog and bird, thus subjecting the dog to a double temptation: check him again: then, when steady, let him get a bit nearer the bird, drop him, move up the bird with his string, then fire more shots—

in fact, do all you know to try the puppy, and then check him patiently every time. An hour or two of such work morning and evening for two or three days will steady the most wilful puppy. The same plan may be adopted for fur, substituting alternately a hare for a rabbit. But above all things shift your ground every time, and do not let your puppy see you preparing your plans. He must come upon bird or fur totally unawares, and in all sorts of places.

Whilst I was writing the above I received the subjoined letter on the subject, and I will deal with it here, as some of my readers may possibly be in the same predicament—a not unusual one by any means :—

DEAR SIR,—I have read with great interest your notes on "setter and pointer breaking." I am trying to break a brace of dogs. I should, and no doubt others would as well, like to know how to treat dogs that are in the habit of running a long way ahead and won't turn to call or whistle, but keep on going, standing momentarily, then flushing and chasing; and when I take them in the neighbourhood of birds—that is, they can always find birds on yonder hill—they leave me in the valley, away they go on the hill, flush and chase, and won't heed whistle or voice, and come back when they like. Would it not be a good plan to have a lad on a pony, with a good whip, to go round them and drive them back to me, I to stop and whistle in the meantime? They won't beat their ground to and fro, but run straight off. I have read Colonel Hutchinson's little book, but he does not explain this most important point. I shall be glad if you will explain this.

Now, the fault described by my worthy correspondent is a most aggravating one, but, fortunately, one which is pretty easily cured in a puppy. With older dogs, however, it is by no means so easy ; but it has been done, and I will explain succinctly the plans which I have found answered best.

First, with puppies. They should be taken out one at a time, and the puppy should have a longish check-rope on. Bring him into a field with the wind in his teeth, drop him, let him start for, say, forty yards, then whistle and check him. If he resists, peg him down, or draw him back to you, and jerk him down ; or, if very obstinate, give him the whip ; but do all this whilst you are blowing your whistle. Repeat this half a dozen times, and you will find that afterwards he will turn the moment the sound of the whistle strikes his ears.

But you must use your own judgment as to the

"TO HO! 'WARE RAIL!"

amount of whipping required. If you overdo it, say
with a timid dog, he will certainly turn to whistle, but
instead of going on with his ranging in the other direction, as you wish him to do, he will probably connect
the whistle with a lathering in store, and slink back to
your heels. On the other hand, if the puppy is very
bold, and you do not impress him sufficiently with the
virtue of the whip and its connection with the whistle, he
will disregard both. Therefore, tact and judgment are
required there, but, if well resorted to, success is absolutely certain. When turning the dog to whistle, you
should turn yourself, and walk in the direction desired,
thereby showing the dog which way you wish him to go.
And the breaker must not spare himself, but repeat the
performance every time he turns the dog. Some dogs
are naturally so wishful to please that they keep their
eyes on their breaker the whole time they are ranging,
and they are so anxious not to lose sight of him, or even
of being too far away from him, that the moment he
turns, however slightly, they bear away at once, and
tack towards the quarter towards which he himself is
advancing. Every puppy who has been well handled
should do that sort of thing—but there are very few
puppies who are well handled, worse luck!
    Well, now, let us suppose a puppy has been worked on
the check-rope until he turns readily to call or whistle;
the next step will be to give him his liberty and see if he
will remember his lessons. If he does, well and good;
if he does not, resume the rope until he does; but if he
seems half inclined to obey it is a very successful plan
to run him with a plain collar or with a check collar
buckled on pretty tight for half an hour or so. He is so
bothered by it that he does not want to get much away,
and turns readily at call, because he thinks you may
possibly want to relieve him. Twiggez-vous?
    Indeed, the principle is well known and sometimes is
acted cruelly upon. For instance, it is a very usual
trick of some dog dealers when a likely buyer insists
upon trying some wild brute of a dog of theirs, to put on
the dog a spike collar, buckled on so tight that the dog
endures perfect misery the whole time he has it on, and
will hardly get away. So that if the buyer wants a
careful animal, the dog will, to all appearance, suit him,
as far as his "going" goes. This is a dodge which is

carried on in the most barefaced manner at the present day, and buyers will, therefore, do well to beware of it. When a man wants to buy a sporting dog, he should in every case insist upon a thorough trial, and he should first assure himself that no trick is used to make the dog appear other than he really is. Therefore, he should first see that the dog has good eyesight, good hearing, good teeth, is free in his action, good tempered, and likely to be serviceable. He should see if the collar is pretty loose on his neck, and that no spike is used anywhere. (Some dealers are very tricky in that way, and have only one or two spikes put on a plain collar, in such a manner that outwardly no sign is visible of any spike being on at all.) Well, all those things being right, the intending buyer should see the dog on fur and on feather, and also tried with the gun, and something being shot to the dog. The reason for all this is that many dogs will stand feather well, but not fur, and many who will stand a gun being fired, if they see anything shot, will run in and have it, generally tearing it to pieces, and sometimes eating it too. So, altogether, a perfectly broken and reliable dog is rather scarce. I have had many hundreds sent me on trial, and hardly one or two in half a dozen turned out satisfactorily, whereas those broken under my own supervision invariably turned out well. Therefore the fault lies in bad breaking.

The plan of sending a man or boy on horseback to turn recalcitrant wild dogs rarely answers. It is always best to use the check-rope, whistle, and whip until the dog is made amenable to whistle, no matter how long that may take the breaker.

Clearly my correspondent's puppies have not been worked on the check-rope plan, since they are not only regardless of whistle and voice, but put up everything they see and chase it. If he does not check these propensities at once and steadily, the dogs will grow into useless, wild brutes. They should be taken in hand singly, until made steady on point and free from chase. Running two unbroken young dogs together is a fruitless and thankless task, and I therefore strongly advise my esteemed correspondent to put them separately through the course of training I have previously described.

In some books on dog breaking the breaker who wants

to train a young dog to back is recommended to get another dog on point, and then bring the youngster close behind him on a check-rope, and force him to drop. I do not advise the same plan, because, in the first instance, there is no occasion for a backer to get close to a point at all. A good backer should stand or drop, no matter how far off he may be, as soon as ever he catches sight of his mate on point. Besides, by bringing the puppy too close to the point, he may possibly get the birds too, and then want to take the point himself—a thing to be particularly discouraged in any dog.

For these two reasons I advise acting as follows:—In the pairing season, when birds lie well, let the lad set a very stanch dog going to find birds, you all the while keeping the young dog out of sight. As soon as the old dog gets a point, bring the puppy in sight—say, from behind a fence—and allow the check-rope to slide gently through your hands. If he begins creeping towards his companion (as some highly-bred dogs will do instinctively), then steady him by voice, "To ho! Back!" gently enforcing the order with the rope until he stands as firm as the dog on point. Keep him there for a few minutes, then signal to the boy to go up to the pointer to put up the birds, and to drop the pointer by voice or hand if he does not readily drop to wing, and you do the very same thing simultaneously with the puppy. Should the latter, however, on being first brought to view his comrade, attempt to start ahead indifferently, for quartering, or jealously, for running up to point, check him sharply with the rope, repeating, "To ho! Back! Back!" and even drop him with the whip if he seems over-greedy to be off.

After several lessons of this sort, let him loose—with the rope, of course—and if he should take the point he must be dragged back to where he should have stood still every time he does wrong, and the whip must be used if he will stand it without any harm.

Backing is a great accomplishment when well performed, but many men, who think they are pretty good judges, have, to my personal knowledge, been taken in in the most barefaced style at some field trials. Indeed, at several meetings one of the very judges was repeatedly sold by a breaker, and to this day he thinks a certain dog is a good backer, whereas to my knowledge he is nothing

of the sort. The dodge is as simple as can be, and some
field trial men have brought it to the height of perfection. One of them breaks all his dogs in such a manner that they will remain stock still wherever they are
as soon as he stops walking. By this means, as soon as
he sees the rival dog on point, the breaker stops
abruptly, puts his hands behind his back, and looks
towards his dog. No sooner does the latter catch sight
of him than he pulls up sharp and stand still—and the
judges give him good marks for excellent backing, and
the trick is done; but in every case he is not backing the
other dog at all, but is simply backing his own breaker.
Another man drops his dogs by hand as soon as the
other fellow has a point—and the thing is done again.

But all this is not what should be called backing. I
contend that, although the whole thing shows great
command over the dogs, it does not prove at all that the
dog would back if left alone to his own devices. Indeed, I know for a fact that several dogs, who have
repeatedly been given credit for good backing, will not
back on any terms if left unchecked to their own way of
acting. Some dogs give no trouble whatever in teaching them to back—it comes to them naturally—and I
think it awfully pretty to see a nice, well-matched brace
of dogs alternately backing one another, as though petri-
fied by the same electric shock. If a dog does not take
kindly to backing, the safest plan to confirm him in it is
to drop him, whenever he ought to back, with the check-
rope, and not allow him to get up again until the birds
have been put up and the other dog has been sent on
again on his quartering. Indeed, it is always desirable
for dogs to drop to wing and gun instead of standing
still, because the less to be seen of the dogs then the better. For that reason I think very large pointers and setters are a mistake. One does not want cart-horses in the
field. On the other hand, the other extreme is to be
avoided, because a "weed" can hardly be seen on the
moors, or in high turnips, or in Essex rank grass, for
instance. A happy medium in size is the thing. And,
taken all round, I think a setter of, say, Lingfield
Beryl's size and style is just what should be required.
There are nose, pace, energy, style, and indomitable en-
durance, and the size is just what I should call a perfect
"workman's" size.

A SPANISH POINTER.

D

Here, by the way, for fear I should forget to mention it, I would strongly advise some breakers to give up their proverbial ash-plants and use a whip for correcting their dogs. Some men are very aggravating with their inevitable sticks, and continually whack their dogs with them over the head and face. Now, nothing is more dangerous. One of my very best working pointers was blinded in one eye by a blow thus administered by one of my men, who would hit him with his ash-plant. The consequences were I lost a "pony," and the man got "sacked," of course; and this was not satisfactory to him or to me. A retriever with a coarse, thick coat will stand a "rib-roaster" with an ash-plant beneficially. Indeed, some of them do not care a rap for the whip, but if the man loses his temper and hits him on the face with his stick, unpleasant consequences may then ensue. On the whole, therefore, I should advise ash-plants to be used with extreme moderation and care, even with retrievers.

When working a brace of young setters or pointers, every expected act of theirs should be strictly enforced. If one of them does wrong, drop both dogs, then keep the one not guilty down, walk up to the other, drag him back by force to where he should have dropped, and correct him. Do not mind trouble. Repeat this every time—fifty times over in a day if necessary—for if you neglect doing so you will never have a perfect brace of dogs. Of course, the two youngsters should never be worked together until, singly, their breaking has been completed. As I pointed out to a correspondent, working two imperfectly broken young dogs is a very thankless bit of business; in fact, it should never be attempted.

Well, then, supposing the two separately act fairly well, take them out together, and start them one on each side, not allowing them to run together side by side, racing one after another jealously, for by so doing they would be sure to flush, and, in the excitement of the moment, possibly chase. If at first they will go on together, side by side, drop them repeatedly until you can send them separately right and left. If one of them flushes, drop both—it will do no harm to the other—and pull back the miscreant. If one refuses to back, do the same thing, drag him back and keep the other down. Above all things, be sure they are both free from chase before bringing them out to work together; but if one should suddenly take it into his head to start after fur it is a million to one that the other will think it the best bit of fun he ever was asked to join in, and he accordingly will join in—with the result that it will give you extra work in bringing them back to their original standard of perfection.

Talking about standard of perfection, some men (who think they know a good working dog when they see one) are not aware, seemingly, that a dog is a sort of machine, which, like all other machines, requires "winding up"—more or less. Some high-couraged setters after a month's idleness or so require one or two days' work to put them right. But some men try a dog without any thought of that. A case in point occurred quite lately. A well-known setter, shot over for four seasons by two different and well-known men, was sent on trial, and he was returned as "worthless." That was the verdict given by the "sportsman" and his "keeper" after a two or three hours' run! And the dog had been idle for four or five months, and they knew it! Now, men like that may say what they like, but I think they will have their work cut out to make people believe that they understand dogs.

These are the sort of men who go on talking about their knowledge of dogs, and how they were nearly swindled out of the value of a dog, and so on, and so on.

There is, unfortunately, no gainsaying the fact that many men do not understand dogs, but wish to be thought experts all the same. They slip the dogs anywhere and anyhow, up or down wind, and expect the dogs to find and stand game, not by scent, but intuitively, so to speak—irrespective of their having the wind or not, or whether they are "strung up or not" for the performance!

Such expectations are perfectly ridiculous. As to keepers, there are very few of them nowadays who understand working dogs—let alone breaking them. I saw a raw one once slipping a setter down-wind in turnips, and when the dog, of course, flushed, he turned round to his master and remarked that "that 'ere dog weren't up to much!"

To his master's credit, however, be it said, the man

was discharged there and then for having obtained his situation under false pretences, and he then admitted having never worked a setter or pointer in his life!

Now, personally, I hold keepers in high consideration. They are, as a rule, a worthy set of men, but to me one who does not understand dogs seems a perfect fool, and I would not have such a man about me—not gratuitously. But there are very many such about, unfortunately. They, however, invariably represent themselves as perfect "connoisseurs" in canine lore and skill, and, if their master knows no better, they play perfect havoc with his dogs and with his sport.

Some men assert that the use of the puzzle-peg is beneficial to some low-hunting dogs. I do not believe in it. If a dog hunts for foot-scent, his nose is at fault, and all the puzzle-pegs in the world will not give him greater powers of scent—any more than a glass eye would improve his eyesight if he had lost the pupil of one of his eyes. It is sheer nonsense. No puzzle-peg improves any dog's style of hunting in a permanent manner, but, on the contrary, if the dog is naturally very fast, it may so hurt him as to make a potterer of him.

The fact is, a good dog will look for body scent if he can trust to his nose. If not, he will potter, and therefore he had better be discarded, for no puzzle-peg will improve him.

The check-collar, however, is useful, not because it hurts the dog, but because it bothers him, and thereby renders him more amenable to discipline. It may seem strange but it is so. Anything out of the common put upon a dog steadies him very considerably; possibly, as I hinted before, because he knows that you can, and possibly will relieve him yourself. The check-collar, by its balls, annoys the dog, and is absolutely harmless by itself—the reverse of the spike collar, which is cruel at all times—but, of course, when the check-rope is pulled the pressure of the balls of the check-collar on the dog's neck is not pleasant. At the same time, it cannot injure him.

Another device frequently resorted to. more especially abroad, for dogs addicted to chasing, is a short oaken stick, fastened to the collar, and hanging in front of the chest. As long as the dog works with composure, the said stick troubles him but little but let him start at full speed after fur or wing, and the thwacks he gets on his forelegs and feet are a "caution," and soon bring him to his senses, even if he is not bodily tripped up by the stick and brought to mother earth with a crash.

Boarhounds and other big watchdogs, who are known to be apt, when loose, to chase strangers, cattle, vehicles, or horses, invariably, in Germany, wear such sticks, and they effectually prevent them from doing as much mischief as they otherwise indubitably could and would do.

In conclusion, I would advise no man to undertake breaking a dog who is not himself perfectly broken. Some men are so excitable, or so impatient, that dog breaking is to them an impossibility. They want to break a dog, and are themselves so uncontrollable that they might well be defined as being quite unbroken. I have seen men, after winging a bird to a young dog, run after the wounded bird with yells worthy of one of Fennimore Cooper's wild Injuns—of course, inducing the puppy to run in too and help in the hunt of the cripple; and yet these very men will wonder next that the young dog will run in when they fire! I don't. As a matter of fact, I think dogs occasionally display a great deal more composure than their masters. It is a curious thing to me that not one shooter in twenty will allow a winged bird to escape rather than spoil a dog. I call upon shooters as a body to testify to this. How many times have they observed a companion yeling frantically and rushing breathless and hatless after a crippled bird, or hare, or rabbit, thereby endangering the steadiness of the valuable dogs which were at the time being shot over? I pause for a reply. No. These men would rather get their four-shilling hare or two-shilling bird and spoil a twenty-guinea dog than lose what they have shot! Clearly, such men are completely unbroken, and are a pestilent example to all well-broken sporting dogs within sight or hearing. At the same time, generally these are the very men who find fault with the dogs if they subsequently should act upon the bad example which has just been set to them. How often have I seen the following scene:—

Two guns and a keeper are out for a day's sport on the stubbles. A brace of young setters, carefully spring-broken, find birds, the brace of shooters advance, up go the birds, down go the setters, and, say, a brace and a

HALF A MIND TO SULK.

half of birds bite the dust, but one of them is a runner. Thereupon the enthusiastic shot yells vehemently to the keeper to come forward with the retriever; then, catching sight of the bird, and thinking he will cut the matter short himself by nailing it, he runs after it, kicking, shying his hat or a cartridge, etc., and the young dogs join in with great gusto.

Results: All the birds within a mile are upset, the dogs will run in ever after, whether the birds fall or not, and the individual—cause of all the mischief—then turns to his keeper with an aggrieved look, and remarks with great dignity that "he does not think much of the youngsters' breaking!" We have all of us seen men of that stamp, and I think my readers will agree with me when I say that it is highly unsatisfactory for any dogs to have to do with such shooters.

I say, keep cool under any circumstances. If you don't, figuratively, drop to your own shot, you cannot expect your dogs to do so. Give them a good example; be steady and cool, and you will be surprised to find how quickly your dogs will take to your ways and show you sport. But eschew the company of all harum-scarum shots. They will spoil your sport and ruin your dogs. Verb sap.

Abroad they teach all pointers and setters to retrieve. (See illustration.) Here such work is almost exclusively reserved for retrievers proper.

I will now take in hand the breaking of spaniels.

FIELD AND COVERT SPANIEL BREAKING.

The working of field and covert spaniels differs but slightly: therefore, the general breaking hereunder explained will apply to the breaking of both. If a spaniel be intended to retrieve, the very first lessons given to him, when he is quite young, should be to teach him to carry. Some people break a spaniel on game first, and expect him to take naturally to retrieving in after life. Some dogs do, but many do not, and even the few who do work very badly in that respect, generally mouthing their game dreadfully, and not infrequently bringing it

to hand in a woeful state, rendering it unfit for the
table. Yet some men call that sort of dog a "retrieving" spaniel.

But, then, some people are born wags, don't you
know! I have often had fifty spaniels sent to my kennels on trial, and but half a dozen or so were really fair
retrievers. The least said about the others the better.
I shall deal fully with teaching to retrieve when taking
retrievers proper in hand, because it is a special branch
of canine education, and it will require somewhat
lengthy explanations.

I shall, therefore, confine my remarks now to breaking spaniels to game and gun, and my hints will apply to
either retrieving or non-retrieving dogs. The first step
is to teach the dog obedience in ordinary matters. He
should be taken out at first on a leash and taught to keep
to heel, then let him run, but with a loose check-rope (in
case of accident), and introduce him to horses, cattle,
sheep, fowls, etc., and prevent him from chasing, in a
summary fashion. Spaniels, as a rule, are very turbulent, but very fearful of man; once licked, twice shy.
I have known many who never required teaching twice
to 'ware domestic animals. Howbeit, no matter how
wild the young dog may be, the rope will render him
amenable to discipline, and if he does not obey orders it
will be not his fault but his breaker's.

Once the dog is well entered to those ordinary animals
which he is likely to meet about farmhouses, he should
be taken into a large, bare field and taught to downcharge. Nothing is easier. Peg him down, drop him
by force; walk away from him, and, if he stirs. force him
down and keep him there until you may do almost anything and he won't stir. When he does that well, put
on a twenty-yards check-rope and let him go on; then
call out, "Drop," and drop him gently at first but somewhat roughly afterwards if he seems inclined to rebel.
This should be practised until he drops readily at call.
But some spaniels are exceedingly cunning. They will
drop as long as the rope is on, but as soon as it is removed they will try on their tricks. In such cases the
whip should be resorted to, because they are wilful dogs,
who are perfectly well aware that they are doing wrong,
but will do it out of sheer love of mischief.

Howbeit, patience and a check-rope will go a long

way. The dog is bound to give way in time and to obey orders implicitly. When he drops, then, freely to hand or voice, let him work perfectly loose, and drop him if he attempts breaking fence. When confirmed in not getting away from the eye of his master (and it is surprising to note how well-broken spaniels always keep their eyes on the gun), the young dog should be entered to fur, and the best plan that I know of is to get a lot of rabbits let loose in front of him by a confederate; but the dog must have the check-rope on, as he is sure to try to have a go at them sooner or later. A gun may also be fired now and then, to see if the double temptation of fur and gun will lead him astray. Practically, however, not one covert spaniel in a thousand drops to gun and to fur. Most people are very well satisfied if the dog simply desists from going after fur after a yard or two, or if he stands still when a gun is fired. I know, in some books, we are shown pictures of four, five, or six Cocker spaniels dropping to gun. It looks well; but we will safely bet our bottom dollar no man ever saw six Cockers in full work dropping all together like machines whenever a gun was fired. I have seen some of the best dogs out in covert, and I have never observed anything of the sort. Oh, yes, we have been told that the dogs would do it—but they did not, don't you see, and that's where the hitch comes in. I have, however, seen, of course, many teams of Clumbers dropping well, but in the open one has a far better control over dogs, and Clumbers are mostly broken in the open. It is, however, surprising to observe the admirable ignorance which some men display. Many who want a spaniel expect to get for £2 a dog that will drop to hand, wing, shot, and fur, and they seem to have no idea of the labour involved in breaking any dog to do all that.

A member of the staff of a well-known paper once staggered me by informing me that he had bought such spaniels for £2 or £3 apiece. I at once jumped at such a chance—who would not?—and offered to buy one hundred on the spot at a fiver each and give my cheque for it: but, alas! like many another careless statement, this vanished into thin smoke. Yet there was a chance for that worthy friend of netting at least £200 by the transaction. But, no! He dropped the subject, and I never heard any more on the matter. Yet this gentleman was an authority, wrote brilliantly on many sporting subjects, but clearly he did not know what he was talking about.

Now, it should be borne in mind that it does not matter what the breed or size of the dogs may be, breaking them perfectly takes just as much trouble. Ah! if broken dogs were only sold by the yard, or by the square inch! Then I could understand that a pointer or a setter should fetch more money than a Clumber or a Sussex, and especially a Cocker! But they are not so sold, and, as a matter of fact, it would take you just as long to teach a small Cocker to drop to hand, wing, fur, and shot as it would to train the biggest pointer or setter that ever ran. Therefore, why there should be such a discrepancy in their prices, and in the estimation in which they are generally held, is one of those things which "no fellah can understand." I know some men who will readily give thirty and forty and more guineas for a good pointer or setter who will not give more than £2 or £3 for a Cocker, and expect him to do "everything but talk," as the saying goes.

Now, that is simply absurd, but that it is so no one will gainsay who knows anything of the subject.

Coming again to our spaniel breaking, I should strongly impress upon spaniel breakers the absolute desirability of having the dogs perfectly secured in their kennels. If spaniels get loose and start on a hunt by themselves when they are young, they will acquire such vile habits as will never be thoroughly eradicated. They will hunt after bunnies, chase them to ground, yapping all the while, and altogether will get so fearfully and pleasurably excited as to long for further editions of the same at all and any opportunities. A self-hunting spaniel is an awful abomination and one may take it for granted that he acquired the habit through neglect and being allowed his liberty somehow, without anyone watching over his conduct.

Spaniels in covert should notice fur, but should only drive it for five or six yards. And here again comes the question: Should a spaniel be mute or not?

I say he should not be quite mute, but he should not keep on giving tongue. I like a dog to just open when he finds and puts up—and that's all. A dog that gives tongue noisily and persistently is useless, but one abso-

WATER SPANIEL AT WORK.

lutely mute in a covert will not make you have all the
fun and sport you ought to have. I like a dog to give
me warning if possible, and I fail to see, as some men
assert, that it drives away all game. It is simply nonsense. I have often in my own woods shot seven or
eight pheasants within a square of, say, fifty or sixty
yards in furze and fern brakes, and they were put up,
one after the other by a brace of Cockers, who "called
out" when they found them and put them up. Then,
if the dogs' voices are so disturbing to game as some
people would make us believe, why did not the six or
seven last birds go when they heard the dogs "talking
to" the first? It is simply nonsense. The fact is some
men get so awfully nervous that the slightest noise
upsets them, and, if they happen to miss—well, then
they darn the dogs heartily, just as if it was the dogs'
fault! I know, when a man is no shot, the dogs are
always at fault, and if not the dogs it is "the sun in their
eyes," or a "twig that hit them just then on the nose,"
or "the ground, which was slippery," or their "coats
that do not fit," or "the whisky overnight," and so on—
but it is generally "the dogs' fault." It is never, by
any fluke, the shooter's—oh, dear, no!

Now, I say that a steady dog who opens on flushing
does a great deal of good, because he "drops" all pheasants within hearing. Of course, if you do not at once
beat your ground, they will trot, naturally enough: but
if you proceed smartly there and then you will have
them right enough—at least, that's my experience.

I have seen birds on the move a mile ahead of beaters,
but they take dogs far more coolly, if they are steady
and well broken. In fact, to me, shooting in covert
with beaters is a waste of good stuff, and those who wish
to enjoy it really and truly should try dogs. I will warrant they will never resort again to biped assistance.

There is a very prevalent notion on the Continent that
Cockers, Sussex, Blacks, and Clumbers, being all classi-
fied there as spaniels (the generic name for setters
abroad), point their game like setters. I constantly re-
ceive letters to the following effect:—

DEAR SIR,—I want a good Cocker (or Sussex, etc.); he must
range well, be firm on point, and retrieve tenderly, etc.

And, of course, I have to explain that they do not

point in the full acceptation of the term, i.e., not in cata-leptic style. Most dogs (even terriers), when coming suddenly upon game or rabbits, make a decided halt before springing them; and if that halt be cultivated and encouraged the dogs will take to standing deliberately on game. Nothing is easier than to teach any dog to thus point—but this is not the cataleptic point of either a well-bred pointer or setter, and it is not always to be relied upon. Some Clumbers, however, which I have owned have pointed almost like setters, and most of them will take kindly to being trained to point. Cockers and terriers, being more turbulent and restless, are accordingly harder to train to stand, but patience and a check-rope, as I said before, will perform wonders, with time.

However, broadly speaking, I should say that, natur-ally, spaniels do not cataleptically point, but that some, in whom exists a natural tendency to do so, are pretty easily taught to do it fairly well.

It is obvious that to train any dog to point simply consists in working him with a rope and checking him when he finds game, until he comes to connect scent of game with stopping of all motion on his part.

I have had several terriers thus pointing rabbits, and waiting until I came up before springing them out of their forms in the bushes or in fern and furze brakes, and most of my spaniels continue to do so. A Clumber of mine, which I sold to Mr. D. some years ago, pointed every head of game he came across. But it is not every Clumber that will act thus.

Generally speaking, however, if a spaniel is well broken to work for the gun—and not for himself. as many do—whether he will point or not is a matter of the utmost indifference, because his master comes to know his ways so well that the moment the dog scents game about the shooter is aware of it, and gets ready accord-ingly. But if the dog is a wild one no sport is possible, for he will dart after his game anywhere and anyhow, and will spoil everything. Some spaniels are excessively cunning. They will gauge their new master most accu-rately, and take advantage of him if they think they can do so with impunity. Some dogs—very steady with their breaker—play the very deuce with a stranger until brought sternly to their senses. If the whip seems insufficient they should be taken to work with a check-thong and stopped short whenever getting excited or unruly. The check-rope should never be made of cord of no matter what thickness, because it would not only rot away very quickly, but its dragging on the ground would soon destroy it. A proper check-rope should be made of five or six long strips of untanned leather, spliced carefully end on, and the splicing should be bound with fine brass wire. Some men advise that a few knots should be made in it every two or three yards or so, and it is obvious that these knots are useful, for, by putting his foot on the rope anyhow, a knot is sure to bring the rope to a check pretty sharply, but I think these knots make the rope wear too quickly, and, after all, a plain strip of leather does not slide very far under your foot if you happen to stand upon it with all your weight.

The thong should be ½in. wide and ¼in. thick, and the raw hide should be really good to be of any use. Such a rope, properly used, and greased at night, is practically unwearable.

To teach a spaniel close ranging, he should have not more than thirty yards of rope on, and he should be shown plenty of ground game, and should be heartily shot over. When a bunny springs up, call out "'Ware chase!" and check the dog. After a dozen such lessons shoot the next rabbit, and stand on the rope in case the dog wants to go to him. If you have young pheasants about, do not fire, but let the dog spring them and drop to every one. This you can make him do readily if you hold the rope firmly and work him carefully. French birds, in rank grass, are capital practice for spaniels, as they have a strong scent, run a good deal, and therefore try the dog's mettle thoroughly.

With regard to working capabilities, there are good, bad, and indifferent spaniels. There are some which, for instance, will never face prickly covert, such as thick furze, blackthorn, etc. Others will go through anything. Those who object to that sort of work are either deficient in experience or else have been in their youth pitched into bushes by some irate breaker—than which action nothing can be more stupid, as it is sure to disgust any puppy. Some men bring a puppy spaniel to a forbidding-looking thick bush, and tell him to go in. The young dog, scenting no game, thinks the man is a fool, and won't do anything of the sort. Thereupon the fellow swears at him, and, seizing him by the nape of the neck, flings him head over heels into the thorniest part—from which the puppy scrambles, howling with pain, as fast as he can, and he is not likely to face anything of the sort calmly afterwards.

Yet such a man coolly represents himself as a breaker! Of course, he says, the puppy will be no good, and it is accordingly made away with—or else sold for show purposes, if good-looking enough. Anyhow, here is a dog deliberately spoilt for work, which might, with proper handling, have turned out a gem of the first water.

Now, facing very hard and prickly bushes is naturally not a very tempting sort of thing to do, and, therefore, if there be nothing to induce the puppy to face it, he will not do it; but let the well-bred keen puppy be taken to a fresh rabbit run into the same bush, and I will warrant he will soon bundle the rabbit out, and think nothing of the job—indeed, afterwards, if any bush is pointed out to him, recollecting the treat he had had previously, he will go in "like a man" to see what is in it.

And in the same way young dogs should be entered to water. Pitching an inexperienced dog into a deep river under the pretext of teaching him how to swim is a dangerous and useless process. Dangerous, because the puppy may be drowned; useless, because he connects water with violence, and, therefore, shuns it. I, however, happen to know a breaker who asserts that he has cured several water-shy dogs by repeatedly treating them to a dose of deep water from a high bank. Of course, it may be all true, but I do not believe it, because my experience is quite contrary to it. That one or two cures may thus have been effected is possible, but that it would answer with every dog is wrong, I know. The plan I advocate is to take the water-shy puppy to a gently-sloping bank, with shallow water deepening gradually into swimming depth, and tempt it to go in further and further after pieces of bread every day. He will soon take to it and forget his fear; but it should be borne in mind that there are dogs who never can learn to swim. It may appear strange, but it is so. They are willing enough to go in, but cannot swim a stroke. They splash about and manage to get out again, but in a swift-running river they would be doomed to get

drowned. I have seen myself a dog of that class. If
he saw any game in the river, he would go for it without
the slightest hesitation, but he had so many narrow
escapes from drowning that eventually his master used
him exclusively for land-shooting.

Spaniels, as a rule, are absolutely full of "go"; they
are always on the move, bustling about, and, accordingly, want a lot of work. Some lazy keepers and
breakers, who do not like work themselves, resort to
various expedients to tame their spaniels; some strap
one of their forelegs through their collar, others load
their necks with heavy leaden collars, and so on—all
plans which are more or less stupid or cruel. Of course,
a spaniel working on three legs will go slower than if he
had the use of four—but that does not train him. It
may temporarily break his spirit by crippling him, but
it does not permanently affect his training. Give such
a dog two or three long days in hard covert, and he will
moderate his pace; but to keep him chained up for a
long time and then suddenly bring him to work is to
expect too much if steadiness is expected of him. I
have known some keepers religiously keeping their
spaniels on the chain from the end of one season to the
beginning of the next, and who, when bringing
them out for the first time, are surprised that they are
wild.

"Won't you be steady, you brutes, you? Here, come
in, will ye?"

And then the poor beasts' forelegs are strapped under
their collars and the lot go hopping about like cripples
until they can no longer stand, when that leg is released,
but the other one strapped up for a change! That is
something like breaking and working!

Howbeit, there are very few lively spaniels which
will work well without a touch of the whip now and
then: but if kept in constant work they are fairly amenable to discipline, and certainly show more sport all
round than any other breed of dogs.

Indeed, with a good spaniel, many men are perfectly
satisfied. A friend of mine in Essex has one such, with
which nothing comes amiss, and from August 1, when
snipe and flapper shooting begins, until March 15, when
every shooting is over, that spaniel is at work, and he is
equally at home in the marsh, in turnips, in hedgerows.

and in the big woods. But, then, the owner is a sportsman, and that is the whole secret of the affair.

When big woods are properly divided by rides, nothing is easier than to prevent spaniels from getting away too far from their breaker. Let their breaker go in with them for each beat, and let two guns be respectively on his right and left in the rides, and keep about fifty yards ahead of the man. Whenever a dog gets too excited and starts after a bunny or a hare which crosses either ride, the shooter who is there at once rebukes the dog by cracking a whip at him, or even by only pretending that he is going to pick up a stone and shy it at the dog. (N.B.—At the same time, be it well borne in mind that under no consideration whatever is ever a stone to be picked up and shied at any dog—such a practice might, and very certainly would, in the long run, lead to an accident, such as blinding a dog or laming him.)

Now, if the shooters are pretty strict in turning the young dogs and, above all, in refraining from killing that ground game which they are in pursuit of, it is wonderful how quickly well-bred spaniels give up such riot. But nothing is worse than taking young, unbroken spaniels for a covert-shooting party, comprising many guns—all more or less "all there" for slaughter. The dogs will get so demoralised by the heavy firing and the many temptations which promiscuous shooting will throw in their way that they will get quite wild, and will go yapping after every bit of fur or feather they will put up. Therefore, to properly train young spaniels for covert shooting, there should be only two guns, with proper instructions to nail only feather, and to keep their eyes and ears open in case a dog tries to cross a ride.

If these rules are properly followed, a dozen such lessons will bring the most ardent young dog to his senses. It stands to reason that if every time he wants to get away he finds someone in his way to drive him back, nolens volens, he will soon come to learn that he must strictly confine his attention to the beat actually in hand, and that he must not chase on any terms beyond its surrounding rides.

There are some men, however, who do not mind a little wildness, and who enjoy chasing immensely. These are "hot guns," always on the "snap" for everything which stirs, and, of course, to them a wild dog which puts up game is not quite so thoroughly looked down upon as he otherwise would be, because they like the noise and bustle, and enjoy every find by sight or by hearing, even if they cannot kill for the time being. I have been with such men myself, and they say, "Oh, yes, Dash is very wild, but he does find 'em, doesn't he?" Well, of course, that may be fun, but it is hardly correct sport.

Clumbers are the easiest spaniels to break. Next to them come Sussex, and finally come Cockers, which generally get tremendous lickings before they will keep pretty steady. I have also had four Blenheims, broken for covert shooting, and they gave me excellent sport. They were obedient and very clever—not over-keen—but yet "all there." They were, however, too small for retrieving; they could not carry a pheasant, usually dragged along rabbits, but were nonplussed by hares. 'Cocks, however, were easily tackled by them, and I must say it was a very pretty sight to see one of these little fellows carrying a fine woodcock as big as himself nearly, apparently; but, on the whole, I was always in a blue funk when killing ground game lest I should bowl over one of the dogs. For bird shooting exclusively, however, they were unrivalled, for they pressed a pheasant so sharply that there was no escape—up he must get if they got at all ahead of him, as he could not double again past them. For 'cocks, I need not say that they were simply splendid, and I never knew them to pass one. Rabbits they put up sharply, but only went after them for a few yards. One thing was, they were dreadfully afraid of punishment, and, therefore, at the slightest call or low whistle, they dropped all nonsense.

Some men when covert shooting like a lot of beaters to be with the dogs, and encourage them to kick up an awful row. I cannot say I like the plan at all. I have hundreds of times been standing in rides, and pheasants have come past me, running, and would not rise, thus spoiling sport, simply because the far-off noise had put them afoot, and all they cared about was sneaking away full speed, and never thinking of getting on the wing. Now, dogs would put up such birds which defy beaters. Therefore, I think all will agree with me that for downright, genuine covert sport no human ingenuity can devise· anything better than the help of good, well-broken spaniels.

WATER-SPANIEL BREAKING.

I now come to water-spaniels. First, as to size, I think a large water-spaniel, say, of the size of an Irish dog, is simply out of the question. The biggest thing a water-spaniel has to retrieve is a swan, and surely it does not require a very big dog to retrieve even a swan, and this performance, be it remembered, he may possibly be called upon to carry out but once in his lifetime. Generally speaking, ducks are the largest birds he has to retrieve. Now, this being so, I say that a very large dog is a mistake, and certainly the old English water-spaniel was quite big enough for all purposes.

The breaking of a water-spaniel is, without doubt, the hardest of any dog-breaking, and no water-spaniel is worth his salt, as regards experience, until he has had a couple of seasons. The reason for this is not far to seek; the dog has to learn so many more things than other breeds of dogs. He must stay ready for flighting, remain still in a punt, he must never open under the strongest temptation, never jump up, never be excited obey signs implicitly, hunt when told, and keep to heel when ordered as well as a perfectly broken retriever. He must also be tender-mouthed, very keen-nosed, strong-constitutioned, plucky, swim for ever, and stand hard winters with equanimity. A dog who does all these things well clearly is a valuable dog, and he cannot learn them all well in a hurry. I have seen very few really good water-spaniels, but I have seen liver retrievers doing their work well. In short, for all-round water work, a good, medium-sized liver retriever is the most generally used nowadays, and I have had wonders myself. I have had several who, the moment I got to my flighting spot, curled themselves up under the reeds, out of sight of birds, and waited there for events with remarkable tact and complacency. A good flighting dog, whether he be a water-spaniel or a retriever, should never be spoken to. When you fire, he should listen for a fall, and if he hears the bird "striking the mud" he should go for it straight, without orders. If he does not, you will lose the bird, because if the bird is dead his scent will soon be cold, and if he is alive he will dive and get away and be a lost bird. The dog who has retrieved a dead bird should put it at your feet and resume watch. But if he has a cripple in his mouth he should only deliver it into your hand, so that you may despatch it. If not, if the dog drops it amongst the reeds at your feet, it is as likely as not that the cripple will manage to give you yet another hunt.

Of course, the proper colour of a wildfowl spaniel or retriever is liver on the back—do not mind about any white on chest or on legs or toes. These things are only show defects; they count for nothing for work. The main point is that the whole upper part of the dog's body is liver, tail and all. And, by the way, a water-spaniel should not be docked. His tail is his rudder, yet I have seen some which were as close-docked as Cockers. Clearly, this is a silly proceeding.

On the other hand, although breaking a water-spaniel gives a good deal of trouble, it is the most entertaining breaking out, but, the dog should be taken in hand young. First of all, he should be thoroughly trained to gun, to water, and to retrieve—of the latter more anon—and when he does all that well he should be hunted on moorhens, or, better still, on flappers if he happens to be just of the proper age for work in July or August.

It is a very good plan to teach water-spaniels to drop to hand and remain down until ordered to come to heel or to hunt. The reason for this is not far to seek. You may be on one side of a stream, whilst the dog is diligently beating the rushes on the other, when suddenly you spy fowl on the wing a great distance off coming straight for you. Now, you, of course, drop at once, but if your dog keeps on working the birds will catch sight of him a long way off, and will swerve out of shot as a matter of course, whereas, if upon seeing the fowl coming you drop the dog and he keeps perfectly still, the chances are great that the birds will keep the line of flight perfectly undisturbed, and, if coming straight for you, you will have a fine shot.

Now, to teach the dog to drop is simple enough, and I

have explained how to do it when treating of setter and
pointer breaking, but to train a dog to stand perfectly
still, even when you move, requires a little more care,
but it is very simple too. It consists simply in pegging
the dog down, and dragging him back to his downcharge every time he is tempted to get up, and you must
tempt him in every way—walking away from him,
crouching in reeds, etc.—and never let the dog rise or
move until you wish him to do so. This is the worst
part of his training, because it requires time and great
patience. Naturally, when he loses sight of you he
wants to follow, and when he sees you stalking away
from him he wants to come to heel to see for himself
what you are after. Some dogs, naturally very keen
after sport, cannot be brought to that pitch of perfection,
for, even if trained to drop when signalled so to do, they
whine with excitement at the expected shot, and thereby
would spoil sport. A dog who whines should, therefore,
never be trusted away from you, down-charged, but
whenever any birds are sighted he should be called forth-
with to heel and dropped there, where he will be much
more under your control and far less likely to whine or
otherwise disturb the fowl.

A water-spaniel should never be worked near water
with his check-rope on. The reason for this is obvious
enough. He may start in pursuit of a moorhen, twist
the rope round some willow tree root, and either hang or
drown, or both hang and drown, himself. Again, a
water-spaniel should never be trusted to cross a river for
beating the opposite side until he is perfectly steady and
keeps as close to the gun as circumstances will permit.
He should keep his eyes ever and anon on his master, and
he should have the sense to flush his birds in your direction. This, a well-bred, well-trained dog will do readily
enough. I have had dogs which, on scenting birds,
would dash round at a jump to cut off their retreat, and
compel them to face my gun and its murderous contents.

One important point in a water-spaniel which is used
for extensive wildfowl shooting is that he should not
sulk. Now, I make bold to say that there are very few
dogs which do not now and then sulk, sometimes for
the most trivial work on hand. I have seen some otherwise hard-working dogs which could never be brought to

A COCKER FLUSHING A WOODCOCK.

swim three times running across a river for dead birds
unless you fire again and again to induce them to go
over, and even then sometimes they did not choose to go
and would not go. This is unaccountable, as, of course,
one would think that a retrieving spaniel would be glad
to have as many birds in his mouth, one after the other,
as he could find. But that this sulking is of frequent
occurrence I call upon all men who do a great deal of
wildfowling to testify, and I have frequently noticed
that this sulking will occur all the more readily if the
dog has had an opportunity of mouthing all the dead
birds which he ought to retrieve. Thus, say, for instance, you put up from a river four or five ducks, and
you kill, say, three with your two barrels, and the three
fowl fall on the off-side on bare ground. You send your
dog over to retrieve them. Just as he is picking up the
first, perhaps one of the others flutters on the ground, or
he otherwise becomes aware of its proximity and sees it.
Well, he drops his bird and goes for the second, takes
that one up, and then sees the third. He drops the
second, and goes for the latter. You swear at him, of
course, and order him to bring it; he does so. Then you
tell him to go over and fetch the others, but he will de-
cline doing so, and possibly will not fetch the third bird
on any terms whatsoever.

I have seen such things occurring times out of number with retrieving spaniels. But poodles—which are all
said and done, but a variety of water-spaniels (as I explained and proved conclusively in an article published
some years ago in "The Field," and reproduced in
"Dogs of the British Islands," by Stonehenge ")—
poodles, I say, never do sulk, if, of course, they are well
broken. I have never seen a wildfowling poodle sulking, and I have seen several which had to retrieve dozens
of birds after one single shot. Now, I call that good
work. But to have a dog which looks at you sulkily,
sticks to heel, and won't go again, when your birds are
dead on the off-side, or maybe are slowly drifting away
to sea on the stream, is enough to drive you wild, and
no wonder sulky dogs do get such tremendous lickings—
which, however, do not improve the state of affairs, but
quite the reverse.

On one of the last days I was on my marsh we were

trying a spaniel which had been sent to me for trial with a very high character, and just as we got to the bend of one of the rivers three ducks got up. I killed two, and my keeper nailed the bird. My two birds fell on the opposite bank: his tumbled into a fast-running stream. The dog swam across, picked up a bird, brought it over, then my keeper took him at a run to the bird in the water, and he fetched it out all right, too; but nothing could induce him to bring over the third duck, though he went three times in succession to it, sniffed at it, mouthed it, turned it over with his nose, etc. . . . And, worse luck, as I stated before, that sort of thing is not at all unusual with ordinary water-spaniels. Some sulkers, if a gun be fired again, will pick up the object of their sulkiness, but this is a proceeding which is fraught with great disadvantages. First, you may upset your shooting by firing thus without anything to fire at; secondly, you waste your ammunition; thirdly, you encourage your dog to run in to gun in your anxiety not to lose your bird. All these things are to be deprecated, and are, to say the least, a great annoyance. But I know of no remedy for sulkiness. If the dog is licked, he will, as likely as not, give up retrieving altogether—thus making matters worse. The only thing to be done is to try what patting the dog will do. Encourage him, make much of him, and possibly he may go on again. If he won't, and you are not inclined to lose your birds, do as I have often done, strip and fetch them yourself. I think I should have made a very good water-spaniel. Joking apart, it is very aggravating to have to do with a dog given to sulking, but there is no certain cure for that defect.

One of the most annoying habits into which a wild-fowl dog may get is that of whining when he nears wildfowl, say, in a punt. The only remedy that I know of is to have a ring screwed in the floor of the punt, and to have two spring hooks on a very short line, one hook slipped on the dog's collar ring, and the other on the floor ring, and the dog is thus securely prevented from seeing anything. Then there remains the noise of the feeding birds, which may so excite the dog as to cause him to forget all punishment and make him whine again in his anxiety. A dog of that excitable temperament is very troublesome, and spoils sport, but after a few good lessons he generally drops it. If he does not, he must be discarded altogether for punt shooting. Personally, I do not care much about having a dog with me in any punt of mine, except I intend punting in a district much cut about by deep creeks. In such cases if you have no dog you lose a lot of your winged birds by reason of your being unable to come up with them quickly. It stands to reason that if after a shot you have to row round a point, whilst you are doing so your cripples are doing their best to get away, and by the time you come up to where they should be, half of them are missing. In such a case a good dog is invaluable, but the puntsman should wear oilskin overalls if he has a dog with him, otherwise he will be speedily drenched.

A good punt dog does not attempt to come into the punt with every fowl he picks up. Mine are taught to bring each bird to the punt, and as soon as I (or my puntsman) takes hold of it, the dog is waved back to hunt for more. However, in many districts a dog is unnecessary for punting. In others he is very handy, but, as I have shown. he must be simply perfection to be of any use.

I now come to

RETRIEVER BREAKING.

Here Watts' words apply most forcibly. He says:

> Discerning, patient, skilful, just,
> Should be the man with whom you trust
> Your dog to break; one that affords
> Not the mere evidence of words,
> But proof that he has o'er and o'er
> Succeeded perfectly before.
> In such a man your dog will find
> From first to last a teacher kind.
> And when its schooling's done you'll say
> You have not thrown your cash away.

There is scarcely a better test of a dog-breaker's ability than his success, or want of it, in retriever breaking.

The first thing to be done is to ascertain if the puppy is likely to be a good-nosed dog. And here prizewinners' progenies should be discarded if the said prizewinners are not also of a working strain. Nothing is more heartbreaking than trying to train a dog whose ancestors have not been broken.

The puppy should be taken in hand early—say, at four or five months old—and first his nose should be tried. If he is deficient in nose he is no good.

Once satisfied that he will do in that respect, teach him to retrieve in play, by throwing a stuffed rabbit skin on grass, not on a gravelly road or yard ; gravel disgusts a puppy and makes him tear the skin to pieces. Take the skin from him gently when he does bring it to you. Do not roughly pull at it—if you do he will think you want to have a game with him, and will accordingly pull too. If he will not bring the skin to you, but jerks it up into the air and catches it, and romps about with it, put a check-rope on the dog and check him every time he shakes the rabbit skin or he tries to jerk it up, then call him to you and pull gently on the rope until he comes to connect the words "Bring it!" with implicit and quick obedience to deliver his load. If, when you tell him to pick it up, he seizes it (the skin) brutally he should be reproved and jerked quietly with the rope. If, when he comes to you with the skin, he keeps a tight hold of it, and won't let you take it away from him, pinch his nose quietly, and say, "Softly, softly."

These lessons sometimes take a long time to carry out. Other puppies learn very quickly. The field where you teach the puppy should be in a secluded part of the farm, where nothing is likely to distract the puppy's attention, and once he begins picking up the skin readily do not throw it, but drop it in the tall grass, then take the dog away some distance, make him drop with the rope, and fire a pistol, loaded, with powder only, several times, compelling the dog to remain down the whole time. Then give him the wind, say, "Hie, lost!" and make him seek the rabbit skin.

This is all right for a young puppy, who will take to retrieving in play, but older dogs require being compelled to retrieve. And for this a different plan should be resorted to. The dog's mouth at first should be opened and the skin put into it. He will, of course, drop it. But persevere, and when he does hold it make him walk with you a few yards, carrying the rabbit skin in his mouth.

When he will do that, you may resort to the re-

TRYING WORK FOR POINTERS.

mainder of the breaking as applied to his younger brother.

Virtually, therefore, a very young retriever is taught to retrieve in play; an older one must be compelled to do so. Of course, you must get birds as well as the rabbit skin for practising them. So far, so good; the puppy now will work to order. The next thing is to show him live game, and plenty of it, and of all kinds. You cannot teach a retriever his business unless he has hundreds of head killed to him by land and by water.

When you first take the dog out for earnest work, have him secured by a short leash to your belt, and never let him move, under any circumstances, as long as he evinces a strong desire to run in whenever you fire or whenever game appears in his sight. In short, a retriever should not be allowed to retrieve game until he is so completely master of his feelings that nothing will tempt him to go in—without orders.

That is the great secret of steadiness in retrievers. And for this reason, a pot-hunting keeper is the worst possible man to have to break perfectly a retriever—because the man is so anxious not to lose a head of game that he will spoil a forty-guinea dog in order to secure a half-crown pheasant, and so on.

The dog should be taken into warrens or coverts where he can see lots of rabbits about, and many should be shot to him; but he should not be allowed to retrieve any until he is quite steady, and remains behind you throughout unmoved. Also he should go with you to the river side and see moorhens flitting about, and see you shoot them, and he should remain quite unconcerned.

When he is perfectly steady, remove the leash quietly and see if he will stand quiet. He should walk behind you, but not tread on your heels, as some anxious retrievers will do, and when he will stand seeing game running about and shot he should be practised for retrieving on a strong winged bird, partridge or pheasant for choice. You should take him to the very spot where the bird fell and tell the dog, waving him off, "Hie, lost! Good dog!" Then he should at once take up the scent and go quickly and smartly and you should wait where you are if he goes well. If he does not at

F

first, go and help him and encourage him; but when he finds the bird stand still and tell him softly, "Bring it."

Do not pat the young dog and make a fuss over him when he has done any good work, because, if you do, he will grow frantic with joy, jump about, probably bark, and chuck your breaking to the winds. Be very chary of your caresses and your punishments with your dogs, and you will find they will pay all the more attention to you.

Abroad they teach all pointers and setters to retrieve, and they do it with a wooden instrument called a chevalette, which is simply a piece of wood a foot long and about an inch thick, perforated at both ends at cross angles, and through these holes two slight sticks are forced, making of the thing a sort of cheval de frise, i.e., no matter how you drop the thing, the large piece of wood is always off the ground, and therefore the dog can always seize it comfortably and no grit can get to it. However, I fail to see the benefit of the chevalet, as it must tend to make the dogs somewhat hard-mouthed, and therefore my plan is better.

Do not allow anyone to interfere with your retriever, and never lend him to anybody. A perfectly broken retriever is a valuable but delicate instrument on which no clumsy hands should play when it is in tune. Some men are very silly in that respect. They will make their retrievers fetch sticks and even stones out of water, and then wonder the dogs get hard-mouthed and run in. Others like them to kill rats, etc., and that brings about the same result.

As a cure for a hard mouth, some writers have advised needles being placed in pincushions, or thorns in rabbit skins. The plan answers admirably, in this way, viz., that if the dog does really prick himself he will possibly never retrieve again.

That's something like a cure!

My plan is to make the dog retrieve the same bird several times, pinching his nose when he delivers it into my hand if he is crushing the bird, and saying, "Softly, softly," in a quiet manner, and taking the bird away from him very gently. If a man gets excited and flurried, or cross, he will never break a retriever properly, for here the whip is entirely out of the question in nine cases out of ten. Therefore, gentleness and patience should only be resorted to.

As to retriever bits, I think they are simply abominations, and I have never worked a retriever of mine with one. They are also useless, unless very large, and then they are troublesome to the dog.

When your young retriever is pretty steady by himself, he should be taken out when pointers or setters are worked, but be sure the latter are perfect themselves, for if they should, for instance, take to chasing they would also spoil your puppy.

Anyhow, never have a retriever puppy loose when other dogs are at work, no matter how steady he may have got when by himself. The short leash should be put upon him unobtrusively, and he should be walked to every point and kept strictly to heel to wing or fur, and to gun.

All these things take time. I consider that no retriever is quite perfect under two seasons' work, although I have had some which, through being constantly out with me, or with one of my breakers, got first rate in every way in one season. This, however, is an exception to the rule. No dog wants more practical work than a retriever to make him perfect. If you kill game over the ranging dogs they should drop to gun, and if there be dead birds they should be picked up by your man, not by the dog—that is, of course, if the man can see the birds. In short, if you wish your retriever puppy to get very steady, he should only be sent on when a runner is on the tapis. To do this, the breaker should stop the ranging dogs, or wait until they have been sent on and the guns have followed them. Then he should quietly walk to the spot where the runner fell, and tell the retriever, "Hie, lost!"

But if you make a young retriever retrieve every bird, the killed as well as wounded, he will come to connect the gun with fetching, and, therefore, will run in, or attempt to run in, eventually, when a gun is fired.

As a rule, therefore, never to be departed from, no young retriever should be allowed to go on retrieving immediately the shot has been fired. Let a few minutes elapse first, so as to insure steadiness.

TRAINING A KEEPER'S NIGHT DOG.

I have very often been asked what were the best means
to be employed in order to thoroughly train what is
called essentially a keeper's night dog (although the vast
majority of such dogs are usually employed by farmers
and landowners as means of protection against thieves,
trespassers, etc.), and I will now give my experience on
the subject. As the chief quality of such a dog must
be a readiness to attack (even without being himself attacked) simply on being told to, the trainer will do well
to choose a puppy descended from parents notoriously
"sour," when he may find his pupil pretty apt to learn
the business. I say he may, for in every litter there are
both bold and timid puppies, and, even when the parents
are both good hands at night work, some of their off-
spring may lack their courage or boldness; still, there
is a chance of getting the right article by going for it to
the right stock. It should, however, be borne in mind
that almost any puppy may be made in time "dangerous," if the trainer proceeds in the right way, which I
will hereafter describe. One thing, however, should be
taken care of when originally selecting your pupils, and
that is, he must be likely to grow large—the larger the
better. A small dog, for an actual battle, would answer
quite as well, and perhaps better—as being less visible
and more nimble, he would be less liable to be hit by
his adversary, whilst he can attack him all round before
the fellow knows where the dog actually is; but it
should be remembered that the user of a night dog never
slips him at evil-doers unmuzzled.

In short, on the principle that "prevention is better
than cure," it is better to have a very large animal,
whose growls alone are somewhat terrifying, and whose
size is bound to impose respect. At the same time,
growling is not sufficient; the dog must be able and willing at any time to "go in" at a nod from his master,
and he must take his death, if necessary, when called
upon to protect him.

Some sentimentalists thereupon will no doubt remark
upon the wickedness of such a proceeding. "Fancy

slipping a ferocious dog at a poor man!" for that is the way these gentry will put it. They don't consider that that man is an idle and dangerous vagabond, loafing all day long, and prowling about all night, in order to pick up what he can lay his hands on, and that, if found out or interfered with, he will as soon as not hit you on the head and bolt.

Therefore the question resolves itself into this: Either let thieves plunder you or else protect your property, and protect yourself whilst doing so. Now, to do the latter effectually, there is nothing better than a properly trained night dog, i.e., a dog well under control, who will at once stop whomsoever he is told to stop, in spite of bludgeons, kicks, knives, etc., and will rather die at his work than cave in. Of course, for such work the more ferocious you render the dog the better; but, on the other hand, too much caution cannot be used. I have known several night dogs who, after having been called upon to do their duty half a dozen times, had taken such a violent fancy to collaring men that, if they had been allowed their own way freely, they would indubitably have worried to death any intruders.

In short, a dog of that sort, when once told to go in and win, gets, for the time being, totally beyond anyone's control. All the evil passions and ferocious instincts of the dog are roused, and you have positively a sort of wild beast let loose. Therefore, in common fairness, unless you are threatened yourself with a very serious attack, or actually attacked, never let go the dog unless he is solidly muzzled. Even then he can do very fair work. The onslaught of a powerful dog, enraged at finding himself powerless to use his teeth, is perfectly irresistible. No man can withstand it, and blows only render the dog more tenacious in his purpose.

The education of a night dog ought to begin when he is quite young. Everybody who has been much with dogs knows that if a puppy be teased when taking his meals he will grow up nasty and sour-tempered. Well, the trainer of the night dog must work somewhat on that principle, but he must resort to teasing the puppy at his meals only when the puppy has acquired sufficient bone and constitution to withstand, bodily, the worry. A growing puppy, systematically bothered whenever he

is eating, certainly gets nasty-tempered, but his growth
is affected, and as size is a desideratum with him, his
meal times ought to be held sacred. But, four hours
after he has been fed, give him a large bone with some
shreds of meat on it, and as soon as he lays hold of it
pretend to pull it away from him: but let him keep it,
and touch him lightly all the while over the face with a
switch. He will get enraged at this, and probably will
fly at you the very next time he sees your hand getting
near the bone. As soon as he does this, to prevent
scratches and bites you must put on gardening gloves,
of the very stoutest leather you can find, and fix them on
tightly at the wrists with straps, so that they cannot get
off your hands. Thus protected, pull the dog's tail, his
hind legs, pinch his ears, and use the switch, while he
has the bone, all the time saying, "Kiss, kiss! At him,
lad!" or some such words, until the dog is beyond himself with passion. Repeat this three or four times a
day, and when he readily flies into a rage you must no
longer continue inciting him yourself, but put him on a
leash, take him out in a field, give him a bone, and then
get someone to come and try to take it away from him.
Hold the dog tight, that he does not escape, for if he
did he might seize the man and injure him. The new-
comer must tease the dog, and always keep out of harm's
way, of course; but a good deal of play must be allowed
to the dog, so that the struggle be made to appear lively.
It will excite the animal; and if the man blackens his
face somewhat and crouches occasionally to the ground,
it will be all the better, for a dog dislikes, above all
things, anything out of the common, and if he could
lay hold of the fellow he would tear him to pieces. In
case he should seize accidentally his arms or legs. it will
be well for the man to have old and roomy clothes on,
well padded with straw, etc., and to allow the dog to
tear the old clothes into rags if he likes, the man all the
time making a great show of resistance. I need not
add that, from the moment the dog goes at a man
readily, he ought to be properly secured when at home
for from that time, were it otherwise. he might bite any
peaceable stranger who came near the house. I would
not advise the dog to be actually chained until he is at
least ten months old, so as to allow his limbs full play;

but he should be kept secluded, and frequently teased by strangers. When strong enough not to get deformed by straining on his chain, he ought to be secured thus at his kennel, and kept there, and people warned not to go too near him.

At this stage of his education his master (or the man who is to use him) alone must meddle with him, supplying him with food and water, and taking him out at night only, and always held, not by a chain, which makes a noise in the stillness of the night, and therefore when in actual work would betray your whereabouts to the evil-doers you want to surprise, but by a stout, sound leash, held usually very short, so as to prevent much play to the dog. In this wise you can always recover from a sudden jerk; but should your leash be a long one, and you were unprepared, in the event of the dog starting forward suddenly, he would certainly floor you and drag you along on your face, in spite of all you could do, for some distance. A heavy and powerful dog of that sort, well fed and ardent to attack, possesses irresistible strength. A night dog of mine once dragged a friend across the yard, and rather "peeled" his nose and his face in the process. The dog had simply seen a stranger at the gate, and, making a sudden rush, carried off my companion to Mother Earth like a sack of chaff.

Another thing to be duly attended to is to accustom the dog to the muzzle and to the spiked collar. The muzzle is decidedly a necessity when you have occasion to use the dog by slipping him at intruders. He must, therefore, gradually be accustomed to wear it. If you were to muzzle him without previously preparing him to it, he would be so annoyed at the unusual impediment that he would certainly stop to try to get rid of it, and would thus waste precious time. As for the spiked collar, it will be well to put it on him only when wanted for active service, because if he were to wear it always he would probably maim himself in his kennel by scratching his neck with his hind paws, when the long spikes would indubitably tear his paws open : whereas, by putting it on only when starting for a probable encounter, he will have no time to scratch, and, therefore, will suffer no inconvenience from the collar. As a means of protection to the dog, nothing is better than that collar. Let the spikes stick out well, an inch or more, and see that they are all pretty sharp. The collar must be very stiff and wide, and the inside well padded with stout leather, so that blow from a cudgel or even the butt-end of a gun could not drive any of the spikes through it. To prevent anything of the sort let the collar be made as follows:—Take a very stout and sound piece of leather and drive the nails (which must be flat-headed) through it; then over the heads of the nails let an equally stout strip of leather be sewn to the first; then fix on the ring and the buckle, and the collar is ready.

With such an apparatus on his neck the dog is master of the situation; for should he floor his man, as he is pretty certain to do, even if muzzled, the man is sure to try what he can do to save himself by seizing the dog's neck with both hands. If the dog has no collar on, or a plain collar, he can thus be held at bay to some extent by a powerful man; but if the collar is spiked the man can neither take a good hold nor hold long, because the dog's violent efforts to get rid of him would tear his hands to pieces. As regards the muzzle, a thief or a burglar or a poacher when caught and stopped by the dog never tries to keep the dog at a distance by seizing his muzzle; he knows better. He knows that his only chance of escape from being worried remains with the soundness of the muzzle, and therefore he takes good care not to meddle with it.

When, however, training the dog, he must not be muzzled, and every opportunity should be given him of tearing to pieces whatever he seizes, and the sham battles into which he is entered with your confederate ought always to let the animal be convinced that he is victorious, and can always get the upper hand of his adversaries.

When the dog has had half a dozen such encounters with the man, he will be ready at any time to run at him the moment you tell him to. You must then go a step further and practise at night in an open spot, such as a ride under covert, etc.

Points of Sporting Dogs.

By Fred Gresham.

It was in 1865 that the first field trial of pointers and
setters was held at Southill, on the property of the late
Mr. W. H. Whitbread, who was the proprietor of one of
the largest estates in the county of Bedford. This
was about the time when, owing to the improved system
of agriculture and the tillage of the land, pointers and
setters were beginning to lose their vocation. Still,
there are many who look back to the period when, with
stubbles—reaped with a sickle—half way up to the
knees, they had shot over a brace of pointers and setters
and enjoyed it infinitely more than the battues which
are now the fashion of the day. To return, however, to
the initial attempt at field trials, it would appear from
the notes of the judges, the Rev. T. Pearce, of Bland-
ford, better known as Idstone, and Mr. John Walker, of
Halifax, that at that time there were some wonderfully
high-class pointers and setters, as the maximum number of points, 100, was allowed to some of the dogs, a
state of things which would not be likely to be the case
in the present day; not, however, that there are not
quite as perfect pointers and setters now as there were
then, but judging by points is not infallible, as it is
most difficult to find any two judges which can agree on
the subject, and it was found, as time went on, that it
was desirable to institute a better system of judging
than that by points.

It may, however, be interesting to give the result of
the last time that point judging was had recourse to.
This was at the field trials at Wrexham, held by the now
defunct Pointer Club, in 1889, when, with a maximum
of 100, Mr. F. C. Lowe's Belle de Bordes was given 98;

Mr. Heywood Lonsdale's Crab, 96; Mr. C. H. Beck's Quits Baby, 94; and Mr. Lloyd Price's Miss Sixpence, 88; this was in the All-aged Stake. The young dogs, however, did not get anything like so near the maximum, as the winner of the Puppy Stakes could only command 66 points. Belle de Bordes was undoubtedly one of the best performers in the field that has ever been seen in England, but she must have had a considerable amount of luck to have reached so near the standard of perfection.

Judging by points has proved a failure on every occasion on which it has been attempted, whether at trials of merit, at work, or when comparing one dog with another in the show-ring. Valuable time is wasted in counting up the points, when a judge who knows his business can decide upon the respective merits of dogs either at work or in the ring much better without having any recourse whatever to figures. A superior plan is that which is adopted at the present time, and is called the "spotting system." We believe that some few trials have been judged in the same way as greyhounds at coursing meetings, but this was found to be even a more undesirable mode of arriving at a correct decision than judging by points, for the second best dog, as often happens in coursing, was sometimes put out of the stake in the first round, which is very undesirable. It may be said that what is good enough for greyhounds, which run for considerably larger sums of money, and over which many thousands of pounds change hands in betting transactions at a single meeting, should be good enough for pointers and setters, and it may also be said for spaniels, now that trials have been inaugurated for them; but the conditions of the competitions between long-tails and those between shooting dogs are altogether different, and the spotting system has become established as very much the better course to pursue when the working qualities of pointers, setters, or spaniels are under consideration.

By the spotting system there is no danger whatever of a dog that shows meritorious work being passed over; the competitors are run together, a brace at a time, as decided at the draw on the night before the opening day. Then, when the first round has been run through, the

The property of Mr. Herbert Mitchell.
Winner, 4th K.C. Derby, Norwich, April, 1908 ;

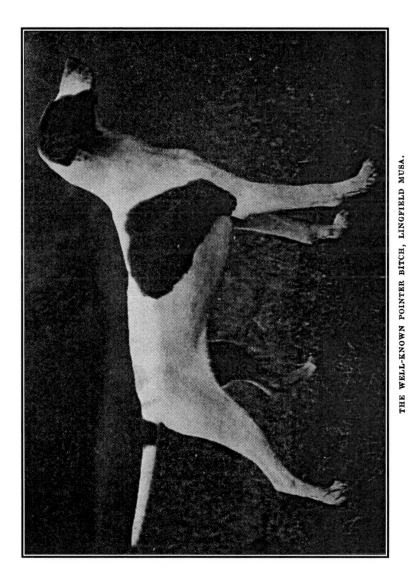

THE WELL-KNOWN POINTER BITCH, LINGFIELD MUSA.

1st, Championship, F.S. Club, Thrapston, 1908 ;
1st, Championship National Trials, Shrewsbury, 1908.

judges, who have taken notes of the work of each dog, decide which have done sufficiently well to be given a second trial, and so on until the prizes are awarded. The judges, of course, are more lenient in the first round than they are in the second, but by the end of the second round a pretty near estimate may be taken of the qualities of the competitors, and the judges are allowed to call up any dogs that have been left in which they desire to see working together. Thus it will be seen that the first and second prize winners may meet without prejudice in the first round, or a brace of dogs; neither of which have shown good working qualities in their heat on the occasion, may not be offered a chance of getting any further in the stakes.

To the inexperienced it may appear a very easy matter to award the prizes at field trials of pointers and setters, and the dogs that get the most points on birds and back the most systematically should take the prizes, and, as a general rule, they are probably correct; but there are many little matters which escape the eye of those who are not thoroughly versed on the subject. Two dogs may be seen running together, and one may appear to have found the most birds, but possibly none but the judges have noticed that the other spotted game on ground that had been passed over, and therefore missed by his opponent. Then, again, there is the question of false pointing, a failing which many of the most highly trained dogs possess; also standing to the scent of birds that have gone. False pointing is brought about by over-breaking, and should be penalised more than it is by judges, as dogs are used for the purpose of saving the legs of the shooter, not to drag him across a fifty-acre field to find no birds when he gets there; and, then, with regard to pointing a stale scent, a really good dog should know that the game is gone. Again, there is a vast difference in the intelligence displayed by competitors, some going about their work evidently with the view of finding game, whilst others hunt about on the chance of birds being in the direction in which they are going. Following is a serious fault. One dog should not follow the other in the same line. When a brace of pointers or setters are sent off it should be in opposite directions, and they should keep within a rea-

sonable distance and cross each other as they quarter the
ground. The faster dog, as a rule, takes the outside
line, and so gets an advantage at field trials, but a clever
dog who is a game-finder will try to get the wind, and
when he has it in his favour will sometimes traverse
the whole length of a field before he turns across; this
is not quite the right thing to do, but it means business.
There is, however, an immense amount of luck at field
trials, and the most brilliant performers will sometimes
make the most unpardonable mistakes, and flush game
which a slower dog would locate; but when everything
goes right the fast dog, provided he has a good nose
and is properly broken, makes a much grander show
than the steady plodder that potters about a few yards
in front of the gun and never runs the risk of making a
blunder.

Amongst the best pointers of days gone by was Drake,
bred by Sir R. Garth, and sold by him for £150 to Mr.
R. J. Lloyd Price, who owned a beautiful bitch in
Belle, whilst Mr. Whitehouse's Priam was also a very
good worker, as also were Mr. Purcell Llewellin's two
setters, Countess and Nellie. From Drake have been
bred several high-class dogs, amongst them being Vis-
count Downe's Bang. Mr. Statter's Dick, Major, and
Rex also won several stakes and made names for themselves; whilst Mr. Price's Wagg and Bang had reputa-
tions both as workers in the field and prize-winners in
the show-ring; but perhaps the most sensational dog that
ever appeared at field trials was the English setter
Ranger, the property of Mr. Cuming Macdona, who
between 1873 and 1877 won seven stakes and special
prizes, and who at times did some extraordinary work,
and was looked upon as a wonderful dog. Mr. Purcell
Llewellin also bred and ran a lot of field-trial English
setters, and so popular has this strain become in America
that his dogs as known there as "Llewellin setters,"
just as Mr. Laverack gained a name in this country;
but for field-trial work it is probable that no one has
produced so many winning setters as Mr. Llewellin,
who in 1884, on the first occasion of special prizes being
given for field-trial winners, at Birmingham, entered
twelve of his setters that had won stakes, consisting
of Count Wind'em, Sable Bondhu, Dashing Bondhu,

The property of Mr. H. Reginald Cook.

FLAT-COATED RETRIEVER, GROUSE OF RIVERSIDE.

A Champion on the Show-bench and a Winner at Field Trials.

Countess Bear, Novel, Dashing Duke, Dashing Beauty, Dashing Ditto, Countess Moll, Countess Rose, Nora, and Norma. For Count Wind'em Mr. Llewellin was offered, and refused, £1,200, and for Countess Rose and Novel £1,000. He has been the winner twelve times of the Brace Stakes at Shrewsbury, at the National Trials, which is looked upon as one of the most important wins, and he won the Kennel Club Derby three years in succession with Sable Bondhu, Dashing Ditto, and Dashing Clinker. With Sable Bondhu, who won in 1882, three others from the same kennel were placed equal, but the first-named was chosen to try conclusions with the winning pointer for the champion prize, which she won. Mr. Llewellin has since then had some high-class performers in Rosa Wind'em, Bruce Wind'em, Nellie Wind'em, Jesse Wind'em, Darkie Wind'em, and Daphne.

In the early days of field trials, Gordon setters were found amongst the prize-winners, but this variety seems to have lost its popularity, as it is now the exception to find even one throwing in its lot with the English or Irish varieties; in fact, Dandy, the champion winner at the first field trials at Southill, was a Gordon, and Rev. T. Pearce also had two good dogs in Rex and Kent.

Irish setters, although little seen at first, have forced they way to the front, and now it is not unusual to find one carrying off the Derby or running well forward in all-aged stakes. For a long time the Irish setter was considered difficult to break, and much too headstrong to be got sufficiently under command to compete at field trials; but this is all altered now, and there are Irish setters quite as stanch and steady as the best of the English variety.

Since the first field trials in 1865, which were promoted by a number of sportsmen interested in the working of pointers and setters, other societies in addition to the Kennel Club, with the same object in view, have sprung up, the National Trials, with their headquarters at Shrewsbury, being the first, and later on the Pointer Club was formed, and trials were held under its auspices, which lapsed in course of time, and then the English Setter Club formed an association with a view to encouraging the working qualities of English setters,

G

to be followed subsequently by the Irish Setter Club. Then what remained of the Pointer Club became associated with the International Pointer and Setter Association, and now the International Kennel Club outstrips all others in the amount of prize money that is offered for competition. It will thus be seen that field trials have become permanent institutions and have greatly increased in popularity since the inclusion of competitions for working spaniels and also retrievers.

In estimating the value of the work of a pointer or setter at field trials pace is a matter of great consideration. A fast dog that quarters its ground systematically, leaving no part untried, at once attracts the attention of the judges. Then, again, the dog that finds game on ground that its opponent has passed over scores heavily, as it is a proof of its superior scenting powers. Some pointers and setters are continually making false points. This is generally a sign that the dog has been over-broken and is afraid that it may flush game, for which it has probably been severely beaten. A clever dog that is running with one that makes false points often runs up a good score to its credit, at the expense of its opponent, as every time it backs a false point of the latter it gains a point in its favour, the reverse being the case with the offending dog. Backing, dropping to shot and wing are all necessary attributes. It is, however, often to be noticed that an old dog that knows its work will pretend that it does not see its companion standing at point, and sometimes will pass in front of it and take the point. This is unpardonable, and, as a rule, leads to the offender being put out of the stake at once. Another fault that is seldom overlooked by the judges is when a mature pointer or setter chases a hare or rabbit. This is, however, sometimes forgiven in a puppy, but never in an aged dog.

At field trials for retrievers steadiness to heel is most important. A no-slip retriever, if perfectly broken, will keep to heel without moving when pheasants or partridges are falling all round, awaiting the order to gather the game. The latter, when found, must be picked up quickly and tenderly, brought back at a gallop, and delivered to the hand without any hesitation. When sent after a winged pheasant or a runner of any

CH. MALLWYD NED.   The property of Mr. J. J. Holgate.

other description, smartness, when accompanied by a
good nose, is very much in a dog's favour, but over-
excitement leads to trouble; the dog gets wild and often
disturbs a lot of game without finding that after which
it has been sent In such cases, when the dog is called
up, another is sent to seek for the same bird, and if the
latter is successful in finding and bringing the game to
hand it is many points in its favour. To run in and
retrieve game without orders is fatal, and to leave the
game of which the dog is in quest and to go after other
that has fallen to the gun after it has been ordered to
retrieve is a fault and is penalised accordingly. A retriever is never allowed to hunt for game; his business is
to retrieve it when it is killed. Not so, however, the
spaniel, which hunts for its game, pushes it up for the
gun, and retrieves it when ordered to do so. The field-
spaniel should drop to shot and not retrieve until com-
manded by the shooter. The Irish water-spaniel is not
required to drop to shot, but to come to heel when the
gun is fired. It would be impossible for a spaniel of
this description to drop to shot when working in the
water or in marshy ground where the rushes are high.
In other respects the spaniel gathers its game in the
same way as the retriever, in the work of which immense improvement is to be seen since field trials for
retrievers were instituted. A decade ago it was the exception to see a no-slip retriever; at the present time no
dog of the breed is considered properly trained that does
not keep to heel when game is being shot without any
deterring influence of any sort.

The introduction at the Kennel Club and other important shows of classes for dogs that have won prizes
or certificates of merit at field trials has done something
towards bringing together the exhibition and the working dog, and has smoothed away to a certain extent the
difficulty that has always existed in connection with
gun-dogs and dog shows, viz., that there is no possibility
of finding out whether a first prize winner is a worker in
the field or not, or of refuting the statements made by
some people that a show dog is of no use for field trials.
With regard to the latter, however, there is now no
doubt that the pointer, setter, or retriever may become
a double champion and be alike successful in both capa-

cities. There have been pointers, and there are now re-trievers, which are winning honours in the show-ring and also in the field, and it stands to reason that any-one who owns a dog would very much prefer one that is good-looking to one that is plain and badly propor-tioned, and the same applies to horses. In many re-spects the points that are valued in the prize-ring dog are also estimated of value in the worker. The judge in both capacities looks for the same points as far as the conformation of the animal is concerned, but the worker must be endowed with specially good scenting power, and he must be well trained; the latter is only an artifi-cial performance.

The points looked for in the show-ring pointer are ele-gance of shape, perfectly laid shoulders, and straight forelegs, with close toes well knuckled up; this is com-monly called the "cat-foot," which is considered by masters of hounds the most serviceable for work; the ribs should be well sprung, loins strong, and quarters well let down, with hocks near to the ground, the stern, which is an important feature in the dog, being some-what thin and carried in a line with the back. There should be no feather either on stern or legs: the head (the indicator of every breed) should be slightly broad and flat at the skull, the muzzle square, with slight flew, the neck clean with ears close to the cheek and of me-dium length. The colour may be liver, lemon, black-and-white, or self-coloured black. The points are estimated as follow:—Skull, 10; muzzle, 10; ears, eyes, and lips, 10; neck, 5; shoulders and chest, 10; back, quarters, and stifle, 10; legs, elbows, and neck, 10; feet, 10; stern, 5; general symmetry, 15; colour and coat, 5. Standards of points have been drawn up by the various special breed clubs, but it has been found impossible to judge by points, as no two judges have ever been found to agree when estimating the points of any dog. The qualified judge takes in at a glance the good qualities and defects of a dog and makes his awards without any regard to the standard of points.

The setter, of which there are three varieties—the English, the Irish, and the black-and-tan (the last-named also known by the name of the "Gordon")—is judged on the same lines as the pointer as regards the

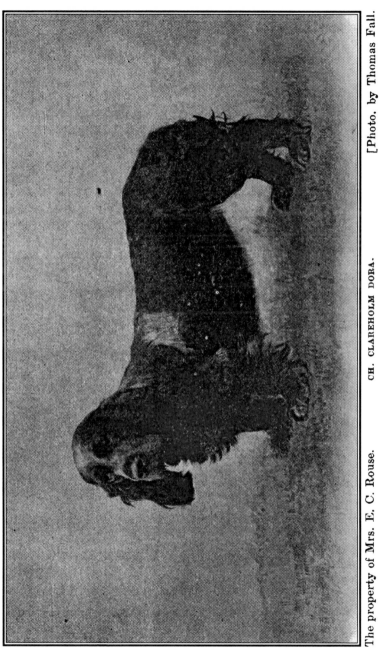

The property of Mrs. E. C. Rouse.   CH. CLAREHOLM DORA.   [Photo. by Thomas Fall.

body properties, but the feet are usually rather flatter and longer, with feather between the toes. The coat of the setter is an important feature; the hair should be soft and silky, without any curl on the body, the hind and fore legs fringed with feather. The head of the setter is unlike that of any other dog; the occipital bone is very pronounced, the skull flat with slight stop, and the muzzle, square, measuring about 4in. from the eye to the end of the nose. The following is the standard of points as drawn up by the late Mr. Rawdon B. Lee :— Skull, 5; nose, 5; ears, lips, and eyes, 10; neck, 5; shoulders and chest, 15; back, quarters, and stifle, 15; legs, elbows, and hocks, 12; feet and flag, 5; symmetry and quality, 10; coat, 5; colour, 5. The Irish and black-and-tan setters differ very little from the English setter. The former is usually a trifle more lathy in build and more cut up in flanks, the latter rather heavier in build all over. The stern of the setter should be carried in a line with the back; it has a heavy fringe of feather underneath, and is commonly called the "flag."

There are three varieties of retrievers—the curly-coated, flat-coated, and the Labrador. The first-named is the oldest variety, and is covered all over the body with small, tight curls. The flat-coated was undoubtedly produced from a cross with the setter and probably the Labrador, which is a much older breed. The flat-coated retriever is longer and somewhat thinner in head and has a smooth coat without any curl, but not quite so smooth as that of the Labrador, which is thicker in skull, and generally coarser all over. The eyes of the Labrador are light in colour, as a rule, but the eyes of the retriever should be dark hazel or nearly approaching black. The Labrador looks nicer when its eyes are dark. The standard of points for the flat-coated retriever is as follows :—Nose and jaws, 5; skull, ears, and eyes, 10; neck, loins, and back, 10; quarters and stifle, 5; shoulders and chest, 13; legs, knees, and hocks, 12; feet, 10; tail, 5; coat, 10; symmetry and temperament, 20.

There are several varieties of the spaniel tribe. The Irish water-spaniel is a tall dog, with curly coat, heavy feather on the legs, with whip tail, the head, which is long and rather tapering at the muzzle, being adorned

on the top of the skull with a fringe of cords overhanging the eyes. This is called the topknot, without which
no Irish water-spaniel is considered pure bred. The
field-spaniel is a long-bodied dog on short legs, and
was up to recently bred for length of body to such an
extent as to render the dog useless for work. Now,
however, it is to be seen more symmetrical in build,
and the very long bodies are being discarded. The field-
spaniel may be black or white, with liver, blue, black,
or orange patches or flecks. The Clumber spaniel is a
stronger dog, heavier in build, with a shorter head, very
square at the muzzle with heavy wrinkles overhanging
the eyes. The colour is white, with orange or lemon
patches, the latter colour being very much the more
valued. The English water-spaniel, like the springer,
is shorter in the body and higher on the legs, and the
Welsh springer is nicely balanced for work, but must be
orange-and-white in colour, whilst the Cocker is a com-
pact little dog, shorter in the back, with a most intelligent expression, and is a very busy worker, with a good
nose. The head of the Cocker is short in comparison
with that of the field-spaniel. The Cocker may be black
in colour or white intermixed with orange, blue, black,
or liver, and the points adopted by the Cocker Club
are:—Head and jaw, 10; eyes, 5: ears, 5 · neck, 5; body,
15; forelegs, 10: hind legs, 10; feet, 10; stern, 10;
coat and feather, 10: general appearance, 10.

Published at the " Shooting Times " Offices,

How to Trap and Snare.

By William Carnegie (" Moorman"), author of " Practical Game Preserving," etc.

A complete manual for the sportsman, game preserver. gamekeeper, and amateur on the art of taking animals and birds in traps, snares, and nets; with numerous illustrations.

Bound in cloth, **2/6**, post free.

74-77 Temple Chambers, London E.C.

Published at the " Shooting Times " Offices,

Fish Farming for Pleasure and Profit.

By PRACTICAL.

Contents : Natural and artficial redds ; the formation of ponds and lakes ; screens and sluices; water supply and aeration ; natural food, aquatic plants, etc.; stocking; rainbow and other foreign trout ; fish passes ; spawning ; how to make a hatchery ; incubation and hatching ; care of alevins and young fry ; concerning rearing fry and yearlings, etc.

Printed on art paper, and beautifully illustrated with photographs and drawings by the author.

Bound in cloth, **2/6** post free.

74-77 Temple Chambers, London, E.C.

Published at the " Shooting Times " Offices,

Camping Out.

BY CAMPAIGNER.

A thoroughly practical illustrated work, dealing with all forms of life under canvas.

Invaluable to the novice or the old campaigner.

Contains expert advice on pitching a camp, together with the most approved methods of drainage, cooking requisites, and everything necessary to camp life.

1/6, post free.

74-77 Temple Chambers, London, E.C.

Published at the " Shooting Times" Offices.

The " Shooting Times " Guide to Ferrets and Ferreting.

By C. J. DAVIES (Author of " The Theory and Practice of Breeding to Type").

A practical treatise on the breeding, training, use, and management of ferrets.

115 pages, with many illustrations.

The most up-to-date book on everything appertaining to ferrets and ferreting.

Price **1/6.** Post free **1/8.** Stiff covers.

74-77 Temple Chambers, London, E.C.

LONDON:

PRINTED AT THE OFFICES OF THE "SHOOTING TIMES AND BRITISH SPORTSMAN," 74-77 TEMPLE-CHAMBERS, BOUVERIE-STREET, E.C.

Lightning Source UK Ltd.
Milton Keynes UK
UKOW040218051012

200054UK00001B/12/A

9 781846 649974